Night Hunt in Kisumu

Night Hunt in Kisumu

and Other Unforgettable Stories from Africa

Richard F. Zanner

Beacon Hill Press of Kansas City
Kansas City, Missouri

Copyright 2001
by Beacon Hill Press of Kansas City

ISBN 083-411-9064

Printed in the
United States of America

Cover Design: Kristina Phillips

Library of Congress Cataloging-in-Publication Data

Zanner, Richard F.
  Night hunt in Kisumu and other unforgettable stories from Africa / Richard F. Zanner.
    p. cm.
  ISBN 0-8341-1906-4 (pbk.)
    1. Zanner, Richard F. 2. Missionaries—Africa. 3. Church of the Nazarene—Missions—Africa. I. Title.

BV3505.Z36 A3 2001
266'.7996—dc21

                                                          2001018077

10   9   8   7   6   5   4   3   2   1

This book is dedicated to my wife and lifelong companion, Valerie, who stood by me with encouragement and support, sometimes fearing for my life but never doubting the divine mandate of my mission. Lovingly, she always provided a beautiful reception in the safe and secure harbor of a cozy home upon my return.

Contents

Foreword   9

Acknowledgments   11

Introduction   13

1. Dawn over East Africa   17

2. The Last Cow in the Village   29

3. Our First Convert in West Africa   35

4. A Story Without End   43

5. The Preacher Boy of Queru   53

6. Night Hunt in Kisumu   65

7. They Labored Not in Vain   71

8. Who Catches a Buffalo with a Mosquito Net?   83

9. A Christmas Message in August   89

10. A Brush with Death   99

11. Scary Moments with a Blessed End   105

12. Slave Station—Outpost West   115

13. A Camel to Last a Lifetime   119

14. A Final Word   129

Foreword

*B*eware! This book could be dangerous to your complacency! Richard Zanner, the African adventurer, has captured the essence of missionary service in this compelling book.

Mined from the heart of Africa's riches, his words speak powerfully for the call of God to win the world. He takes the reader from Idi Amin's haunting tyranny in Uganda to the rapidly changing world of South Africa. You will witness the zealous aggression of modern Islam and the paralyzing power of centuries-old tribal religions. Experience with him an unnerving night on an island in Lake Togo where the drums of voodoo worship fill the African darkness. It was an adventure that resulted in our first convert in West Africa.

The challenging mixture he presents brings electrifying clarity to the daunting issues Africa presents to the world.

Having walked side by side with him through dangerous areas in genocide-ravaged Rwanda and in the warring new Democratic Republic of Congo, I can testify to the fact that danger has been this man's frequent companion. All that being so, he has not been dissuaded from his purposes, for he is confident he never walks alone. In fact, this faith-tested missionary has embraced Jesus Christ, the ultimate Missionary, so effectively that he moves fortified with powerful promises that carry him through fearful moments.

In flying many miles with Richard Zanner, riding cross-country in rickety vehicles with him, eating with him at campsites near a roaring fire beside a river swarming with crocodiles and fearless hippos, I have experienced the heart of a man sold out to Christ and His unshakable kingdom. Somehow his conversation always comes around to the central issue of conquering Africa for Christ.

The Church of the Nazarene has been fortunate to be represented by this valiant soldier of the Cross. His life in Africa offers a parade of captivating experiences born of his hands-on approach to ministry.

These chapters yield the reasons why this leader was chosen to expand the church's work on the heart-stealing continent of Africa. Each chapter is a treasure, each story a new opportunity to feel the heartbeat of a man and his mission. Read on and feel the pulse of a continent still throbbing with need, still hoping that someone will come and finish the task of telling the fascinating story of redemption and love.

I trust that you, too, will be caught up in the suspenseful journey of Richard Zanner, a missionary God used to change Africa.

—Paul G. Cunningham
General Superintendent
Church of the Nazarene

Acknowledgments

I want to thank my secretary for 20 years, Kitty Voges, for faithfully keeping the regional office running smoothly during the many times of my absence and for making that extra effort to type the manuscript pages of this book in her free time.

I would like to pay tribute to a fine team of field directors, Don Messer (Southern Africa), John Seaman (West Africa), Eugenio Duarte (Central Africa), John Cunningham (East Africa), Ken Walker (Southeast Africa), and Theodore Esselstyn (Educational Services). Without them and the host of African leaders, giants of faith, it would have been impossible to advance the cause of the church in this manner.

Finally, I would like to mention Professor Leah Marangu and her husband, John, for their outstanding contributions in the field of education and in helping to establish Africa Nazarene University.

Introduction

*People need significance in their lives.
Without it, they are no more than vegetables
with arms and legs and hands and feet!
Significance in life is derived only
when our efforts are directed outward
and provide a lasting foundation
for meaningful development.*

After recovering from the shock of having a preacher next to him, a man sitting next to me on an airplane flight over Africa said to me, "How do you prepare to change this world with a book [the Bible] and a prayer? Isn't this something that belongs to another age?"

"No," I responded. "In fact, it's Cooper, Twain, and Forsyth translated into reality. If you want to see excitement, adventure, and life from the front row—this is for you. If you prefer the routine of teacup and coffee-table monotony, stay away—you would only subject yourself to the risk of cardiac failure."

Suddenly he wanted to know more. He asked questions and eventually became so fascinated that he asked about the qualifications for the personnel we were looking for.

Of course, that was just the opposite of what I expected. But I was able to share about the power that compels us and the grace that keeps us.

Missions today is not a boring part-time job for pious, white-collared, stiff-necked dignitaries; instead, it's for men and women who are prepared to trust God and are willing to test His promises to the limit, walk in faith, and brave the forces of evil in their ever-changing camouflage.

On the following pages I have tried to paint some of the experiences and incidents—serious and humorous, God-inspired and man-applied—that confront the missionary of the new millennium.

Having recently retired from 20 years as regional director of the Africa Region of the Church of the Nazarene, I feel privileged to have worked with a team of committed spiritual giants, indigenous and expatriate. They have all bought into my vision and have been consumed by my burden, my passion, and the opportunities that so freely present themselves.

The focus is on people—men and women, boys and girls, for whom our Lord went to the Cross almost 2,000 years ago. The burden does weigh heavily, but spiritual passion provides the fire as God shows the way.

A little boy in Kenya who obviously enjoyed an apple I had given him turned to me, eyes quizzically turned up as he munched away, and said, "Uncle, does Jesus also give apples to children?"

"Jesus will show you how to grow an apple tree—there will be tons of apples for you. But you and I will have to dig the hole and put the seed in. Then we have to do the watering and the pruning."

"And what does Jesus do?"

"He'll make the apples grow."

There it is! Shall we try it? In this book you will learn of many different ways of planting and watering. Don't be content to sit idly by. Get up and plant some apple seeds!

His Charge to Me
(Based on Ps. 2:8)

Ask thou of Me, so speaketh God,
  Trust Me to keep My Word.
It is My staff, My holy rod,
  The message you have heard.

The nations steeped in sin and shame,
  The people on this globe—
You are to be the holy flame,
  The answer to their hope.

This earth you own, this land ahead,
  Entrusted to your care,
Rule gently, justly, in My stead—
  You are the heavenly heir!
                    —Richard F. Zanner

1
Dawn over East Africa

Courage in the spiritual world is not to walk blindly.
It is to hold on to God's promises while
using good sense,
exercising good judgment,
and listening to the still, small voice
of reassurance from within.

The lonely road south from Mbale, Uganda, meeting up with the main road from Tororo to Kampala in Uganda, will remain unforgettable for me. An extended long and boomerang-like curve, no meandering, but monotonously dragging through the marshy plains of this part of the country, it impacts the weary traveler as if he or she were at the end of the world. Oh, how he longs for a tar strip instead of the bumpy track with these deep potholes. Rain-washed, crusty crevasses in the dry season will turn into swamps when it rains. I was given to reflection, wondering how long a car as old as this Toyota in which I was traveling would last in this terrain.

The year was 1983. I was on my first exploratory trip to east Africa as regional director of the Church of the Nazarene in Africa. Spying out the land for possible entry of the church was the purpose of my trip.

Although it had been only a few days since I had touched down at Kenyatta Airport in Nairobi, it seemed like an eternity already. Used to the fine road system of South Africa with its well-marked streets, its superhighways with smooth concrete or tar surfaces, I found the contrast nothing short of a nightmare.

My first stop was at the Hilton Hotel in the center of Nairobi. Here was a touch of class, with the friendly smile of the well-groomed, red-uniformed doorman, and delicious cuisine prepared buffet style on a long table with white cloth and pink flowers. I could not have felt better. As I enjoyed my meal, I began preparing myself—bracing myself—not knowing what would await me during the next few days.

Kenya and Uganda were to be my first destinations. These two countries lie side by side, sharing one common history but having drifted so far apart that it would indeed be difficult to find a common denominator except for the warmth of their people and the beauty of their landscapes.

Kenya—the name already exudes an exotic flair. Game reserves like Masai Mara, Amboseli, and Turkana drift through the mind as do the sail-fishing and scuba-diving resorts of Mombasa, Malindi, Gazi, and Shimoni. The economy of the country, while not altogether stable in first world terms, is relatively solid on the continent.

Christian churches abound in urban areas. But what used to be almost friendly competitive shoulder-rubbing with the Muslim world in days gone by fast became a more volatile and confrontational encounter as Islam aggressively began to make inroads, especially in rural areas. This is very noticeable as one travels east toward the Indian Ocean. Arabesque architectural arcades with their flowing intermingling lines blend with the Nubian-styled caftans of the people. The traditional fez, in contrast to the uncovered heads of other Africans, rounds out the picture, proclaiming Arabian domain.

Islam has a peculiar appeal to African people. Its rather placid existence is far more comprehensible than the more outreach-based, less-compromising faith of Christianity. Islam has no racial bias and is able to embrace traditional beliefs much more easily than Christendom. The danger lies in the rather quiet but very determined encroachment through lifestyle, family ties, and culture. The Church of Jesus Christ has to take its stand. The challenge is to make its impact by loving, caring, and life-changing values without seeming to destroy tradition. That's not always easy.

The Uganda of 1983, in contrast to Kenya, still bears the scars of Idi Amin's reign of terror. Hardly a family, certainly not a single village, had been untouched by war and the macabre "ethnic cleansing" doctrine of his regime. Although more Christian in their outlook on life, the people beset by the sins of the past spawn little life and show an almost complete lack of hope during the beginning 1980s in Uganda. The economy was shattered. The once-renowned fruit basket of Africa dried up to be a mere shadow of what it had been.

Uganda struggles with low self-esteem. Hungry, disease-ridden bodies with drooping eyes, hopeless stares, and blank resignation confront you when you try to make conversation with the people of this land. One can see a turn toward the better today, however, and some believe that things will improve within the next few decades.

These were our two countries, Kenya and Uganda, that were to be our next target for church expansion in Africa. I carried out my plan to buy a map and to put my survival kit into a small carry-on bag. Then I negotiated with a Nairobi taxi driver a price for a week's worth of driving, and off we went: north to Nanyuki, heading toward Eldorete, then crossing the border into Uganda. I would cover the east portion of Kenya after my return from Uganda.

I rode through Tororo at a snail's pace with a huge crowds milling about, which proved to be a test of patience. The open market was a picturesque, colorful, and loud experience. Not having seen another European for some time, mine was probably the only white face, I mused.

I spent the night in a small, smelly, noisy African guesthouse, at which I met the first Ugandan who was unintimidated enough to talk at any length with me. This old man, sitting like a beautifully carved statue at the entrance, displayed that very characteristic African expression. It was a blend of pride and dignity in his eyes, giving me a glimpse of the former nobility and grandeur of communal life. He spoke to me of days long gone by. I had to get used to his accent as he began to explain about his people. As dusk settled, I sat and listened, fascinated by his story.

His father had been the headman of a village. There were three wives and 21 living children. Each of them had specific duties and chores. The girls had to tend the gardens, fetch the water, sow the seeds, harvest the fruit, and cook the meals. The boys tended the animals, were schooled in weaponry to hunt, and were taught how to use knives for carving images of animals, people, and huts.

The old man talked as if all of what he had experienced as a teenager were yesterday. I learned how they hunted crocodiles up in the lake by Katakwi. I also learned how they taunted a herd of elephants by coming as close as stone-throwing distance and then quickly disappeared into the dense bush when the elephants turned. This had gone on several times until one day the old herd bull, seemingly losing patience, led a couple of younger males of the herd into the village, trampling 14 of the huts to pulp.

The old man also told me about the day of the massacre when government soldiers attacked his village. His face changed to a stern, sad, faraway look. His recounting was so vivid that for a moment I believed I could hear the yell of the attackers as they stormed and the shrieks of their victims becoming faint whimpers as they were indiscriminately slaughtered. The stench of putrescence in the air had mingled with the nauseating, sickly sweet smell of blood.

The old man had lost both parents plus 15 of his 21 brothers and sisters that night.

The reality of Africa began to dawn on me. The stark presence of death, the thin line between happiness and grief, between the laughter of playing children and the sob of a mourning mother, became very apparent. Beauty here and cruelty there. Africa—secretive, mysterious, unpredictable.

It was this old man who encouraged me to drive north to Mbale and then to take the road down to join with the main road again, crossing the Victoria Nile, which would become the Albert Nile and eventually the White Nile. This was indeed the land of explorers and discoverers. This was the land of adventure, of risk, and of reward. How fortunate I was to be able to traverse it!

Having followed the old man's advice, we had made our way north. The countryside was breathtaking: exhilarating sunsets, village settings like something fresh off a painter's pallet. Turtles along the road and the last-minute flight of yellow-billed hornbills provided an enchanting backdrop.

I stopped my musing and meditation when my driver began getting restless. Scanning the dashboard, I saw why. The temperature gauge was up beyond the red, and steam was seeping from under the hood of the car. A solitary acacia umbrella tree, just off the road, became our target as we stopped. A cloud of steam escaped as the driver lifted the hood, and what we first thought to be a broken thermostat turned out to be much more severe damage. We gave ourselves an hour and a half, refilling the radiator with our mineral water and leaving only one liter or so as a last reserve for drinking water—but all to no avail. The engine would not start again.

What now? Here we were stuck out in the middle of nowhere in the center of Africa. Images of Livingstone and other explorers played havoc with my mind. How much farther was it to the main road? There was certainly no traffic where we were, and even the main road was frequented only by heavy truck traffic, mostly food supplies from Kenya to Uganda.

We worked on the car until it was almost dark, but neither my driver nor I were mechanics, so we decided to give it up and find a village in which to get shelter for the night.

After walking about 30 minutes, we saw some huts—a very welcome sight. The fascinated look on the faces of the people there will remain with me forever. When had they last seen a European? Speaking Kishwahili, the trade language of East Africa, my driver explained to them what had happened. They shrugged their shoulders, offered us some water to drink, and then invited us for the evening meal. On inquiring how far it would be to the main road, I learned that it was about an hour and half on foot.

There I sat that evening in the middle of the African bush.

What a sudden change! A little earlier in the day, it had been a most enjoyable trip for me as I thought about the hardships of the great explorers while I rode on shock absorbers and in an upholstered seat, a pack of cookies on my lap and water in my bottle. Now I felt as helpless as they must have felt at times— exposed to the unknown, vulnerable to numerous hazards, at the mercy of those whom they might encounter.

It was then that I recalled and told myself with reassurance that I was on God's business, and He was with me. Surely there would be a way out. God doesn't need road maps. He doesn't need motor mechanics. He isn't confined to transportation systems and infrastructure, nor does He depend on food and water. God the Almighty was my rod and my staff.

A middle-aged man approached me, obviously feeling sorry for me, and offered me a bed for the night in his home. I accepted gratefully. This became my first night in a strange African village setting.

In the three years of my assignment in Africa, I had slept in hotels, in guesthouses, and with European families in South Africa. But never had I slept in a hut without a window, where the door was an opening three feet high with a reed mat rolled up that at night would be released to hang down like a blanket. I had never sat in darkness with one solitary candle lighting up what was to be my night quarters. I remembered the night in Giyani, South Africa, a year ago. But there, at least, I had a mat. This time it was dried cow dung, hardened and polished.

Entering the humble abode, I could not make out, as best I tried, what else there was besides me. I noticed some divisions, but I saw no chair, no table, no cot. I groped on hands and feet, careful not to bump against anything. My host had pointed out a place for me, and I crawled toward it. I wondered what else, alive and crawling like myself, would share the hut with me that night.

It took a long time to fall asleep. Africa's nights are special. Magic and almost unreal sounds fill the darkness. In the distance was the laughter of a hyena. *Rest for some and mealtime for others,* I thought. Crickets all about, even beside my sleeping mat. I refused to look at my watch. I just wanted to forget where I was and what it was all about. I just wanted to drift off. But it was exactly this urge that kept me awake. I had a good chance to pray—and I prayed that I would eventually fall asleep.

Africa goes to bed with the sun and rises with the sun. So very early in the morning, I awakened to normal village noises: roosters crowing, hens cackling, children talking, fires crackling. It was only through the slits and cracks high up where the grass roof was joined to the poles that sunlight began to filter through. My eyes, now being used to darkness, made out shapes of boxes and buckets and sticks in one corner, as well as items like calabashes and shelves in another corner.

I also noticed that I had not been alone in the hut that night. My host had slept in one of these other divisions, but he was up and out already.

I rolled up the reed mat at the door and was greeted by beautiful sunshine as only an African morning is able to present it. The anxiety, the fear of the evening before, was all erased in a moment. With the yellow orange light pouring out like glowing lava flooding the ground, the shadows receded, and hope returned. Not all was lost, and again I was reminded of my Lord's presence.

Now in the light, I could read. I wanted to speak with God before facing the people and my situation. I took my Bible and felt that I wanted to read one of David's encouraging psalms. So I opened the Book of Psalms and thumbed through them. I wanted to really find a word of encouragement for my situation. I looked, reading here, reading there, doing the things that, as a pastor, I told my people not to do. Searching for a fleece, I eventually stopped at Ps. 13: "How long, O LORD? Will you forget me forever? How long will you hide your face from me? How long must I wrestle with my thoughts and every day have sorrow in my heart? How long will my enemy triumph over me?" (vv. 1-2).

This did not help me very much. I got a hold of myself and decided to continue with my "normal" Bible readings. God was with me, and I determined to throw myself into His hands.

I opened Isa. 51, which was my reading for the day. And there it was. Just what I needed—not a paging through the Bible, not a search for what would fit, not a page-thumbing fleece, but God speaking:

> Listen to me, you who pursue righteousness and who seek the LORD: Look to the rock from which you were cut and to the quarry from which you were hewn; look to Abraham, your father. . . . When I called him he was but one, and I blessed him and made him many.
>
> The LORD will surely comfort Zion and will look with compassion on all her ruins; he will make her deserts like Eden, her wastelands like the garden of the LORD. Joy and gladness will be found in her, thanksgiving and the sound of singing *(vv. 1-3)*.

"Thank You, Lord!" That was all I could stammer. *Everything will come out all right,* I heard the Lord say. *Take courage, Richard.*

When I came out of my dwelling, the lady of the kraal served me a cup of tea. Where did she get tea from out here? She was so thoughtful and had a friendly smile while handing me the dented and beaten mug. As I sat there sipping away and chewing on a piece of dried bread from my survival kit, a group gathered around me. Many of the people just sat down. Word had gotten around—they came to stare at this strange visitor, this foreigner with the white skin who suddenly made his appearance in the village.

For the next three days, this was my daily routine: up at daybreak. A chat with the Lord, then with a friendly family, especially the children. Then a walk to the main road. Sitting next to the road for a couple of hours trying to attract the attention of one of drivers of the passing trucks—they came very rarely. (Most did not stop, and the few who did stop could not offer any help.) In the afternoon the long walk back to the village and the warm reception there.

Washing was another "discovery." I received a bucket—I found out only the second day that the girls carried the water from the river for approximately two miles. The "wash cubicle," or bathing area, was made of dry reed and grass with plenty air cracks. The toilet facility was part of it, a hole in the ground with 10,000 or more flies coming out when a user scuffled into place.

However, the designer doubtless had black skin in mind. White skin, shining through the cracks, attracted so much more attention, evidenced by the giggling children who gathered every time I made us of the facility.

The evening meal consisted of ground cassava root, cooked with an onion-enriched tomato sauce and some green vegetable. Grilled or fried bananas and a sour milk broth served as a kind of dessert. Bedtime followed right after sundown.

After the second day, I began to feel at home. These warmhearted people made it easy for me to live among them. I felt I had almost become a member of the family. I stopped shaving, and by the third night no thoughts of other creatures sharing my sleeping place bothered me anymore.

On my walks to the main road, 14-year-old Barnabas accompanied me, clad in a pair of shorts and an old T-shirt with numerous holes in it. His shorts, more a two-legged loincloth, were somewhat too long and too wide, held up with a piece of string around his waist. The T-shirt displayed the words "Yours forever" in faded colors across the chest. He always carried a stick in one hand and had a self-made slingshot, consisting of a wooden tree fork and two rubber strips from an old tire tube, stuck in the side of his self-made belt. He was barefoot and always cheerful.

I learned a lot from Barnabas. He shared with me about life in the village. On the three days of school each week (he was out for school break) he walked two and half hours each morning to a bush school and two and half hours back home each afternoon. He would start out with three of his brothers (the girls had to stay home and attend to home duties). As more boys from other villages joined them along the way, the group gradually swelled to about 20 by the time they reached the school.

I asked him if he liked his name and if he knew what it meant. "They call me Bani," he said, and I figured that this must be a Ugandan abbreviation for Barnabas. He didn't know what the name meant, so I told him the story of Barnabas in the Book of Acts and that it meant "encourager."

Our long walks gave us ample time to converse, and he seemed very interested in what kind of a man this New Testament Barnabas really was. He asked many questions and gave me ample opportunity to explain Jesus and His love and salvation. The third morning we prayed together on the way to the main road. He was ecstatic when I told him how the Lord called his namesake to preach and, with Paul, was sent by the Church to proclaim the gospel. We became friends.

In the meantime, my driver, who had found accommodation in a neighboring hut, had worked on his car for two days. By the third day he gave up again and joined Barnabas and me standing at the main road.

It was on the fourth day in the afternoon that a truck driver returning to Kenya was willing to take me along. It was quite a sacrifice for him, for he had to wait until I went back to the village, gathered my belongings, and said good-bye to the family and to my many new friends. By the time I returned to the main road, it was already dark.

I promised my driver friend that I would stop in the first town where I could find a workshop and pay for someone to come back to him and tow his car in. I had given him an extra $250 before leaving, over which he was extremely delighted.

It was in Bugiri, approximately 40 kilometers east, where we found someone who was willing to go back and help him. I paid another $100, gave directions, and then made my way back to Nairobi with the truck driver. This gentleman was not only kind but a Christian, too, and we had good fellowship along the way.

I stayed in touch with my bush family through a communal post box address they had given me. It would take two and a half months for them to get a letter from me and two and a half months for me to get an answer from them. I sent each member of the family a beautiful Bible in Kishwahili. To this day they all have a very dear spot in my heart and a special place on my prayer list.

Update: Seventeen years have gone by since these events

took place. God has blessed our church tremendously. The work in Kenya started in 1985 when I requested missionaries Harmon and Beverly Schmelzenbach to move from Namibia to East Africa. From Kenya the church expanded and spread to Tanzania, to Uganda, to Rwanda, to Zaire (now the Democratic Republic of Congo). A Bible college came into being, and a university—the first university of the Church of the Nazarene outside the United States—was established. As I write these lines, we have nearly 70,000 Nazarenes in East Africa and almost 500 students enrolled in Africa Nazarene University in Nairobi.

It's a different world now. Missionaries have settled, indigenous leaders have emerged, and it keeps on going.

As we go back to 1993, however, 10 years after the above events, I received a letter from Barnabas sharing with me that God had called him and that he wanted to be an encourager like the New Testament Barnabas to whom I had introduced him when he was 14 years old. He told me further that he would now be studying for the ministry.

He did. Today he is a pastor of a little congregation out in the bush and has a wonderful wife. They have two children.

The words of Isa. 51, my Bible reading on the first day out at Kutali Village, have become another pillar of my faith: "Look to the rock from which you were cut and to the quarry from which you were hewn. . . . When I called [Abraham] he was but one, and I blessed him and made him many. The LORD will surely comfort . . . ; he will make her deserts like Eden, her wastelands like the garden of the LORD. Joy and gladness will be found in her" (vv. 1-3).

Situations can be uncomfortable for the moment—but oh, if we could only see behind the scenes at times. There would be no more room to fret.

God is at work. He never slumbers. He is never absent. He never goes on vacation. He's accessible 24 hours a day, every day. I know, for I've experienced Him!

2
The Last Cow in the Village

*Whatever you did for one of the least of these . . . ,
you did for me.*
—Matt. 25:40

$\mathcal{T}$he southern subcontinent of Africa twisted in agony, suffering from a seemingly never-ending drought. The rainless skies and the sweltering heat had lasted for more than six years. Fauna and flora had paid a high price. In the Kruger National Park of South Africa, the world's largest game reserve, thousands of animals had succumbed. The formerly green bushveld of southern Africa and the usual lush and green savannahs stretching as far as East Africa had become brown and dusty patches. Life had slowed down. People moved in slow motion. Sleepless nights resulted from the slightest noise that resembled rain. One would wake up, hasten to the window, or rush to the entrance of a hut to see if heaven at last had become merciful. On discovering that the noise originated from other sources, the person would stagger back in disappointment to the bed, mattress, or reed mat and try to go back to sleep, twisting and turning, perspiring and wishing for a breeze, eventually falling asleep again after another false alarm.

By 1984, suffering had spread across countries, borders, villages, and towns like a spark igniting a firewall. Nature writhed in pain. Food had become scarce. Reservoirs, wells, and other water systems were dry. Prices skyrocketed as the shelves of food warehouses and supermarkets emptied. While this was hard for city people, the poorest people in the rural areas suffered the most.

Word reached the African Regional Office of the Church of the Nazarene that the Nazarenes in Gazankulu, in the old South Africa (today part of the northern province of the country), were "at the end." We had approximately 30 congregations in that area, and I had not yet had the opportunity to visit there. Gazankulu was very much "out of the way" from Johannesburg. However, I now felt that this was not only an opportune time but also a nudge from heaven to go there.

It was a beautiful African daybreak when I took off from Lanseria Airfield in a hired Beechcraft Sundowner. How thankful I was that I had taken the initiative in 1981 to earn my pilot's license! Not only did I enjoy these solitary moments in the air, leaving dust, dirt, and bumpy roads beneath me, but I was also able to save time and energy, winging my way across Africa. The world looked much more fascinating from "up there," and somehow I also felt closer to the Lord.

My destination was Giyani, the capital of Gazankulu. Coming closer, flying with no beacons or help from control towers, I used compass and wristwatch with an aeronautical map, just as I had learned. Aviation in Africa was still not easy. Desert, jungle, and bush challenged a pilot to the hilt, demanding constant use of the basics where there were no airways, but also rewarding him with exhilaration that comes when one's limits are tested successfully.

Two hours and 25 minutes later, I wondered where and how on earth I would find a city out there. Arid, dry bushveld stretched as far as the eye could see. Yet my watch told me that it was time to go down. I gave my blind call to alert other possible air traffic in the area on frequency 124.8 and began my descent. Then I saw the "skyline"—a few bleached houses, a gas station, a hotel, the marketplace, and the parliament building. This was typical of how the South African government in Pretoria tried to develop centers in the faraway resettlement areas of the country. On one hand it was remarkable how the government daringly provided infrastructure, but on the other hand it was deplorable that people were not asked or invited, but ordered to move away from the great city centers and left to carve out a living under almost impossible conditions in the rural areas.

Touching down on a dusty strip, I taxied to the edge on the northern end and parked the airplane, using my tent pegs to tie the craft down. I wondered when the last aircraft before me had landed here and when, perhaps in days or even weeks, the next one would arrive. Traffic was sparse out here.

Rev. Nhyati from the Giyani church was there. He welcomed me with open arms, clearly in awe to see the regional director of the church arrive like this, virtually out of the skies. His warm and friendly smile helped me overlook and forget his somewhat shaggy appearance. It was hot, very hot, but as a pastor and true to African custom, he had a jacket and a tie. The jacket was patched on one side, and the tie had also seen better days. The shirt collar was worn, obviously having had different owners in the past, while the trousers were about three sizes too big. Two blue tackies adorned his feet, but I could see only one sock.

We then made our way in his 16-year-old pickup toward town. None of the window cranks worked, and consequently a layer of fine red African soil with the consistency of sifted flour settled onto the dashboard and everything else.

"Reverend One-Sock," as I nicknamed him inwardly but lovingly, did not stop talking. What a wonderful brother he was! He felt that the most important agenda was to give the regional director the history and a current update of his church.

I met with his congregation soon afterward. Although it was a Thursday morning, most of them had gathered at the church building—little or no work was available to them during these severe drought conditions. They welcomed me with the beautiful, rhythmic stances of Africa. Poorly clad and thin, but clean and with an expression of pride in their smiling faces, they were easy to love and respect.

In the early afternoon, after a prolonged meeting with his

church board, Rev. Nhyati noticed my concern for the people in the outlying areas. "Do you want to visit one of these churches?" he asked.

"I would love to. Is it possible for you to take me?"

"Of course. The only problem is that it would be too late to make it back in time for you to fly."

"That would be fine with me. Where would we sleep there?"

"The people in the village would gladly put us up—Africa always has an extra mat."

Little did I know what he meant by "mat." I was to find out that night. In fact, it became my first experience to sleep in an African hut on a reed mattress.

We took some clean water, loaded four of his men on the back of his pickup, and were on our way. Three hours later, longer than it had taken me by air from Johannesburg to Giyani, we arrived. What a commotion our arrival caused! It seemed as if the whole village was part of a special welcome committee. They cheered and chanted, and when they saw that there was also a white face, they gave us a reception I had never experienced. Indeed, this became the first of many of its kind during my 20 years as regional director in Africa. It would have graced a king, I thought. What beautiful people! "Thank You, Lord, for letting me be part of Your kingdom out here."

As predicted, we were invited to stay and accepted. Rev. Nhyati organized an impromptu worship service under what had been a big tree but now resembled a type of stage prop with trunk and branches but no leaves. The church would have been too small for all the people who came to attend.

They sang. Rev. Nhyati prayed. I preached from Heb. 10:35-37—"Do not throw away your confidence; it will be richly rewarded. You need to persevere so that when you have done the will of God, you will receive what he has promised." My topic: *God will not let us down.*

I talked about the sustaining grace of our Lord. I encouraged them with illustrations of answered prayers and admonished them to trust God, who always keeps His promises. In my heart I resolved to back up my sermon with aid for this area. Indeed, I thought, I was there by appointment as a messenger and agent of God.

That night, in a meeting unforgettable to my dying day, we sat around an open fire in the village plaza. The clan chief had given another speech, expressing his appreciation for the visiting guest. Rev. Nhyati prayed a prayer of thanksgiving, and then dinner was served. The men squatted in a circle close to the fire. Immediately behind them were the women, the old ones first, most of the young ones being busy at the outdoor kitchen, where maize had been stamped in ceremonial wood kegs and then cooked on an open fire in huge black kettles under a big cashew nut tree. A young girl came around, towel over her arm and a dish of warm water in her hands. She knelt before me and asked me to wash my hands and dry them on the towel. I replaced the towel over her arm, and she went on from one person to the next. This custom of open-air hygiene is prevalent throughout the African continent where people eat with their hands. Other girls brought a dish with cooked maize or "stiff porridge," and I was taught how to use my right hand to break off a chunk (was that ever hot!), dunk it into the next dish (a sauce of tomato and meat), and eat. The others followed in very orderly fashion. The food was tasty, although different from what I was used to.

I noticed the children somewhat in the background behind the ladies. Looking into their hungry eyes, observing their big bellies, and noticing the shine of red in the normally black hair, I realized two things. First, this dinner was an impromptu special occasion because of my visit and all but a "usual occurrence." Second, these people were starving badly. The children suffered from kwashiokor, a disease of malnourishment. Its symptoms were red hair and bulging, bloated bellies.

It suddenly dawned on me that while I was the cause of happiness for the village on one hand, on the other I was the cause of less for tomorrow and thereafter.

As I ate, and as I participated in this unusual experience, I was given to reflection and began to ask questions. My good brother Rev. Nhyati was so helpful, such a kind and good teacher. Patiently he gave me guidance, and I learned that indeed my visit was so special that they had slaughtered the last cow in the village. Whereas once cattle were moved from pasture to pasture by young herdsmen, village boys aged 12 to 18, these animals had either died or had been slaughtered one by one to feed the people. Maize, the staple food in the area, had been rationed a long time ago, but tonight was an exception.

Did I ever feel bad! I engaged the chief of the village in conversation, asking questions. He called a young man, speaking Tsonga to him, and the man disappeared. About two minutes later he came back holding something in his two hands. I learned then that this was the stomach of the last cow that had been slaughtered—its contents were gravel and stone.

I confess that I had a sleepless night. It was not only my unusual bed—the reed mat—and the stars of the sky, which I could see through the door opening, that kept me awake.

The next morning, after an emotional farewell, Rev. Nhyati, his four men on the back of his pickup, and I made our way back to Giyani airstrip. A few hours later, I was back in the comfortable surroundings of my office and still later in my home, where my wife was waiting with a fine dinner: a beautifully roasted chicken with salad, rice, and a dessert of Bavarian mousse. We thanked God for His goodness and especially included the people out there in Gazankulu.

It was not too difficult to organize a truckload of food, dried milk, mealie meal (maize), dried meat, and salt for our people in Gazankulu. But more than that truckload, this experience became the spark that ignited an initiative in Africa to create the Department of Compassionate Ministries. In time, it became more than just a feeding service for people. It became a ministry in itself, helping our people across this continent to use the Joseph principle of Egypt, looking ahead and planning for the days of famine in the days of plenty, thus learning to provide for themselves.

For me personally, it became a milestone of determination to build a church in Africa that would encompass preaching of the Word, educating the mind, and taking care of the body.

3
Our First Convert in West Africa

He who never tests his limits will never discover the opportunities of his world.

It was my third day in the country of Togo. I had come in from the Ivory Coast, the fourth country on my 1984 exploratory trip to West Africa. I had found many open doors in the four countries I visited—Senegal, Liberia, Ivory Coast, and Togo. Many unforgettable adventures lay behind me. When would we be able to begin pioneering the church there?

The night transfer from the airport to the hotel in the city of Lome, the capital of Togo, became an adventure for me. Having negotiated a price with my French-speaking taxi driver, he lifted my suitcase onto a roof rack and tied it down with some homemade sisal ropes (the trunk of the car would not open). A piece of furniture tied to the passenger seat next to the driver prevented me from sitting there, and since the two back doors could not be opened, I was kindly and with an innocent smile requested to climb over the driver's seat to the back of the car. There seemed to be no other taxi or transport in sight that late at night.

The 40-minute journey was slow, deliberate, and bumpy. Only one of the headlights worked, but the beam was directed to the side of the road. Potholes prevailed, and each time we hit a big one, the driver would turn around to me and smilingly offer a melodious "Pardon, Monsieur." I learned quickly that if I wanted my driver to turn his head back to the road again, I would have to immediately respond that all was well with me. The obvious result of this ride was absorbed by the suspension of the car as well as by the back of my anatomy.

Our drive through the dark African night introduced me to a colorful activity. The streets through the villages and townships were lined with food hawkers, usually women behind little stalls whose only illumination were candles and miniature petroleum lights. Their dim shine spooked over what was being prepared on rusty grills and indented pots, to be served in little dishes. I wondered about all of these diverse smells and cooking activities. We stopped the car. Making sure the driver was at my side—I did not want my suitcase to disappear in the night with a car that had lost its passenger—I clambered over the front seat again to inspect the stalls, their smells inviting, their looks less inspiring.

The background noises were unusual: women's chatter, chickens cackling, disco music blaring from handheld cassette players, boiling fat hissing when diverse insects were put into the frying pan. I saw displays of smoked monkey, chunky crocodile pieces, and bits of yam. The palm-sized portions of yam were from a root approximately two feet long, boiled to a white pulp. All the time I could see shadows and more shadows, like spooks dashing across the street, especially when I diverted my gaze from the stalls to the other activities around. I was reminded of someone speaking about "the heart of immense darkness" in Africa as I beheld the activity. Unforgettable images filled my mind.

We made it to the hotel. I checked in for a good night's rest. The next morning I bought a map of the country, negotiated a three-day price with a cab driver, took my specially prepared travel bag, locked my suitcase in the hotel room, and off we went up-country. Our journey took us to Kpalime Sokade, Tara, then south toward the Benin border through Bassila. After three days, almost back in Lome, we arrived on the southeast shore of Lake Togo. Surrounded by palm forests, with yam fields and coffee plantations to the north, a beautiful landscape opened up before us. I did want to make Lome before nightfall, anxious for a shower, fresh clothes, and a proper bed after these days of fascinating but tiring travel throughout the country. I knew I would never forget this trip. It had indeed been a wonderful experience so far.

By this time, my driver and I had struck a unique communicating relationship that would have amused my family, especially my wife, Valerie, had she known how it went. To her, I was the one who always understood everybody, was always in control, was apparently able to master every situation. But here, helpless and strange, I was talking with hands and feet and everything else—a real circus!

Valerie didn't even know which countries I visited and where I was at the moment. Our church headquarters for the continent were situated in South Africa, and all communication to that country had been severed for political reasons. I had flown into West Africa from Paris and would fly out to Europe again. I knew that at this time only her prayers and mine meeting before the throne of God, her thoughts and mine bridging the gap between there and here, could be the solitary link we were able to enjoy.

I was taken out of my thoughts when my driver, Alfonse, pointed to the far distance across the lake, trying to explain that there was an island there.

"This is where it all started—Togo, my nation, my country," he explained.

Would I be interested in a little boat trip before the final home stretch? I judged the distance, thinking that somewhere down at the shoreline a motorboat would be available, and said yes.

We rode down to the banks of the lake, high reeds on the left side and small, bushy, little swamp islands on the right. Alfonse said that after we found a boat driver to hire, he would wait for me in the car and read the French New Testament I had given him three days ago.

"Nothing wrong with making this trip by myself," I thought. I nodded agreeably until we came around the last bend. There I saw my transportation. It was not a motorboat. On the contrary, it was a 10-foot-long dugout pulled up onto the bank. An 18- to 20-year-old young man lay next to it in the sun, fast asleep. The monotonous sound of softly splashing waves on the pebble beach was interrupted by the crunching noise of our foot soles. The boy woke up, rubbed his eyes, and started grinning. A customer! I was too proud to back out of it now, so I negotiated a price, my driver interpreting. Then I wished Alfonse good reading, noticing his smudgy finger on the pages of the Gospel of John, and departed.

Very slowly, much too slow for my liking, we moved out of the reedy area into deeper water. "Make the best of it and enjoy it while you can," I thought. Sitting in front of the hollow "tree-cruiser," balancing my weight with one arm to the right and one arm to the left on the edge, Praow (the boat navigator) stood behind me and paddled, humming a rhythmic, staccato tune as he took two strokes to the left and then two strokes to the right in monotonous fashion. As he moved the paddle from one side to the other, water would drip into the "passenger compartment." He requested me to remove the water from time to time with an old soft drink can cut open to form a two-and-a-half-inch-deep container.

As we moved out into the lake, I kept my eyes on a group of hippos on the left side that seemed to enjoy the water more than I did at the time. "Africa at its best," I thought.

After about 10 minutes, Praow tipped my shoulder and motioned straight ahead. As we came closer, I recognized the nose of a crocodile. Motionless above the surface of the water, it looked like a piece of debris. As we came closer, it slowly moved away.

After three hours and 5 minutes—much longer than I had expected, we reached the island. For the last 20 minutes or so, I had heard drums and singing—rhythmic, melodious, the unmistakable sound of Africa.

I felt that I must be one of the very few white visitors who had found his way to this seemingly forgotten place, for as soon as we had landed and I had jumped over the front to the shore so as not to wet my feet, about 50 people came running down to the water, waving their arms, women ululating in high pitch (a shrill staccato wailing sound made with rapid tongue movement while exhaling air sharply—traditionally used by African women as a form of applause), men following in a more dignified way. I stumbled, almost falling to the ground. My legs had been bent in an abnormal position for three hours. I stretched like a wild cat getting up in the morning. The people interpreted this as a greeting.

Soon I found myself in the middle of the group, shaking hands, and then the whole group shuffled up the bank to the village with me in the middle as if I had been expected, or as if I were a long-lost member of the community who had returned. I was given a place of honor, received a calabash filled with water as refreshment, while two of the girls peeled bananas, kneeling before me to present them, smudgy fingers leaving visible prints on the fruit.

I refrained from drinking but thanked everyone profusely. After this initial welcome I noticed that my arrival seemed to have interrupted some kind of ceremony. I was reminded that today was Sunday. As they took up their positions again, drums found their rhythm, and shakers, small and large, swirled through the air. Voices began chanting, and sweaty naked bodies moved, sometimes slower and sometimes faster, eventually whirling around as if they were made of rubber.

The shadows grew longer, and dusk settled on the scene. I thought about that long stretch back to the other side of the lake and looked nervously to Praow. He was happily chatting away with a young girl while I wondered how I could end my visit to the village in a dignified way. Suddenly the shakers stopped, the voices fell silent—only the drums continued their rhythmic beat. Six girls, no men, began to sway and bend their bodies. I realized that they were in a trance. I had read much about voodoo and now had the "privilege," for the first time in my life, to experience a live demonstration here.

This went on for a long time. Night settled down. Four fires were lit while drums and dancing continued. I was becoming increasingly uneasy. It was then that an old man dressed in full regalia came out of a hut, a live chicken in his hand. He shuffled in an unusual dance step from person to person.

The six girls, still in a trance, almost like a backdrop to the unfolding scene, looked as if they had no bones as they twisted and bent in every direction.

After the old man had made his rounds, giving every person in the circle a chance to touch the head of the bird, he lifted the chicken and held it by the wings with his left hand while his right thumb and first finger formed a loop around the neck. With a sudden twist and pull, he severed the neck from the body. The dead fowl's legs moved. Wings tried forcefully to lift the body while a fountain of blood squirted. With a wide circular motion, the old man made sure to reach every one of the onlookers, allowing them to also enjoy a splash of blood.

"These people needed God more than anything else," I thought. I was reminded that the voodoo practices of the Caribbean had their origin in these parts of West Africa and that especially Togo had a good portion of animistic and traditional religion. The markets in this country are stuffed with fetishes for all walks of life. Jesus needed to be introduced.

I also received my portion of blood splashing, and that gave me the energy to call it quits. I got up as silence settled on the scene. Frustration mounted within me since I was unable to communicate with the people and share what I felt I had to tell them. So I offered thanks in my own tongue. They did not understand, but I knew that God would. I lifted my arms to heaven and began to pray for this village, for this island, for this country. Everyone listened politely until I had finished. As I began to walk down to the water—by now it was eleven o'clock—taking Praow by the arm, the whole group followed and started their chanting once more.

What a long way back it was! The impressions of the last few hours had remained with me. My pulse was still racing. My heart still stirred with emotion. How and when and who would be able to bring the Word of the saving grace of Jesus to these people?

As the dugout slowly moved out across the lake, I kept on praying and wondering. A clear half-moon sent a beam of light across the water, reflecting a sparklike display on the waves, and I suddenly thought of the crocodile we had spotted on the way out. The group of hippos on the west side of the shore came to mind. My thoughts raced. They went back to my wife, to my family—what if an angry hippo nudged this dugout? It would spell the end of Praow and me. Valerie would not even know in what country I had died or disappeared. I would just kind of fade out of existence with no one knowing what happened. I pulled out my army pocket knife, which I always carry with me, opened the blade, and held onto it until I almost got a cramp in my hand, the knife giving me at least some comfort. But in retrospect, how ridiculous! Yes, I was going to sell my life as dearly as I could, but at best it would have been a mosquito prick in a hippo hide had that happened.

It took three and a half hours to get back. At last this emotionally charged day seemed to come to an end for me. As we pulled the dugout up onto the gravel, I wondered if my driver was still there. Praow walked up with me to where we had left the car. Sure enough, Alfonse, stretched over two seats, was fast asleep, faithfully waiting for me. Never could there have been a more beautiful sight. Exhilarating thoughts of a warm shower, a clean table, a good dinner, and a comfortable bed waiting for me in about an hour and a half or so upon my return to Lome came to mind.

When we woke Alfonse, he beamed his smile from one ear to the other, welcoming me back in French and then proceeding to tell a story. I could hardly believe my ears. How much more could I take? By now it was 2:45 in the morning.

Apparently God had blessed Alfonse's soul while reading the New Testament. I stood there, not quite understanding what he was trying to share. He talked so much and so fast; I understood only a word here and there. Eventually he asked me if I would pray with him, and only then it dawned on me: While I was on my expedition to the island, Alfonse had found peace with God!

The three of us now knelt beside the car. The drums, the trance, the hippos, the crocodile, the lonely ride across the lake all faded away as we lifted our voices to God. Alfonse prayed in French, I prayed half in German and half in English, but God understood it all. A child was born. A new name had been written down in glory!

Togo was unforgettable. Later, as I departed from the Lome airport, walking through customs, I looked back and saw Alfonse standing behind the gate with big eyes, smiling, waving the jacket I had given him as a farewell present. He was our first convert in West Africa. God blessed my soul. Togo became a target for the Church of the Nazarene. So much darkness, but so much light available—light that dispels the gloom.

4
A Story Without End

We have improved our structures,
We have broadened our resources,
We have streamlined our systems,
And we stand on God's promises.

Now for a bold, visionary, and people-focused
approach that would turn our efforts into growth.

Another very hot day was looming. Early in the morning, as we began our district assembly on the Zambia North District in Central Africa, the warm air was already vibrating, distorting contours on the horizon. Not a breeze was blowing.

During the second hymn came a shuffle at the door as a group of children came in. Among them was Lunde Simbeye, approximately six years old, being assisted by some others as he made his way into the church building. It was my first meeting with Lunde.

During the following years, this boy became very special to us. As a baby, he had fallen into a fire, the plight of many African children in rural areas where life revolves around an open fireplace. He had been badly burned—the scars on his arms and legs had begun to ulcerate and hindered muscle tissue from developing normally. As Lunde grew older, his limbs began to pull and to restrict full movement, causing excruciating pain. The scars—ugly-looking, ragged lumps—created further handicaps that eventually prevented him from being able to walk. The prospects for the future, at best a dismal handicap, at worst a life leading to a slow and painful death, were disheartening for him and his family.

Helped up to the platform by his friends, Lunde awkwardly tried to take his place in the children's choir. He wanted to be part of everything that was happening that day. His squeaky little voice certainly was very audible. After the business sessions of the morning, I inquired as to this child's condition and learned about his background.

"What did the doctors say about all of this?" I asked. I was told that apparently nothing could be done for the boy in Zambia. Health care was almost nonexistent. The family had taken him to a doctor repeatedly, but all this man could do for Lunde was give him some pain tablets and tell about the remote possibilities of advanced and very costly health care, possibly in other countries.

A plan formed in my mind, which I discussed with missionary Rev. Lowell Clark. I asked him to get me some photographs of the crippled body with the burn scars and a letter from the doctor describing the condition in medical terms.

Upon return to South Africa, I submitted all of this to our family doctor for further counsel. He advised that we should see a specialist and made the necessary appointments for us at Baragwanath Hospital in Johannesburg. He gave us some hope for helping Lunde but mentioned that it would probably be a matter of repeated operations and much expense.

When we met with the specialists, they confirmed the initial advice from our doctors. They would have to see the boy, however, in order to examine him more thoroughly to be able to make a firm diagnosis after proper examinations.

The ball was now in our court. We asked our district superintendent, Minnaar Zwane in Soweto, if he could find a place for mother and child if we would bring them down from Zambia. He volunteered to take them as special guests in his own humble abode.

I shared this story with some of our church members and in prayer meetings of different congregations, and faithful Nazarenes eventually provided money so that we could make the arrangements for Lunde and his mother to come to Johannesburg.

At last the day arrived. They embarked on their first flight, climbing up the stairs of the huge jet airliner that was to take them from Kitwe via Lusaka to South Africa, a four-hour journey.

Their reception in South Africa was great. Missionary Rose Handloser waited for them at the airport and introduced them to the people at the regional office and at last to the hospital.

The medical staff at Baragwanath Hospital was wonderful. The doctors even volunteered to do the operations free of charge so that the expenses could be reduced to hospital care, medication, and air travel to South Africa. However, a lot of money still had to be budgeted for various trips over a couple of years so that the necessary medical work could be adequately performed.

About four years later, Lunde and his mother sat at our dinner table one evening and expressed their gratitude to God and the church for the way they had cared and looked after them. Indeed, a miracle had happened. Lunde was a different boy. His vivacious spirit was contagious.

I will never forget the evening when, in saying good-bye to us, he stretched out his little arms and put them around my neck for a big hug—something that would have been impossible a few years earlier with his arms contracted, bent out of shape, and virtually dysfunctional.

But this is not the end of the story. A few years later I was back in Zambia for a meeting with missionaries and district superintendents to discuss strategy for the Church of the Nazarene in that great country. It was then, virtually out of the blue, when Zambia North District Superintendent George Kaputula shared with us some exciting and moving news.

A Nazarene layman from our Kitwe church had contacted Rev. Kaputula sometime before. The layman had come originally from Tanzania, one of the East African countries. He had married a Zambian lady and had become a strong layman in the church. He informed Rev. Kaputula of a group of five Holiness churches in his home country who showed great interest in the possibility of affiliating with the Church of the Nazarene.

Rev. Kaputula was burdened by what he had heard and shared that burden in a prayer meeting one day. Shadrack Simbeye—Lunde's father—began to enter the scene. He had become a successful businessman in Kitwe and as such approached Rev. Kaputula, saying, "The Church has done so much for us, our family, and especially our son Lunde. We would like to do something in return."

He then went on to suggest his willingness to finance a trip for Rev. Kaputula to meet with these Christians in West Tanzania. Rev. Kaputula gladly accepted. He and members of his advisory board undertook this 600-mile journey, meeting with the leaders of these congregations, preaching in a number of churches, and discussing Nazarene ways. After their return, they reported how good they felt about the doctrinal and ethical standing of these five churches. They had shared with these people in Tanzania that affiliation with the Church of the Nazarene would in the first place mean responsibility and accountability in all areas. They fully accepted this.

Rev. Kaputula then contacted the regional director and invited him to take a trip there. Brother Simbeye would pay for the expenses. That visit would enable the church to take any necessary further steps.

We arranged that Rev. George Kaputula and some of his men would come from Zambia and Rev. Harmon Schmelzenbach and I would come from Kenya to meet up in Mbeya, Tanzania. We wanted God to guide us in our decisions.

All of this became another milestone in the ongoing development of the Church of the Nazarene in Africa. This venture into Tanzania, completely initiated and financed by Nazarene ministers and laypeople from Africa, became a striking example of a developing church.

Yes, the Body is maturing and is increasing quantitatively and also qualitatively. It is taking its rightful place along with the church in the developed areas, the first world countries, and the globe. Probably only those who live and minister in

Africa can fully appreciate what this means. The financial sacrifice attached to such a venture, within an economy such as the one in Zambia, the burden to bring others into the fold, even across national borders—all of this was something never heard of before. It caused us to rejoice and to thank God. Emmanuel—God with us!

The unique link of Christian people in South Africa giving money for a crippled boy in Zambia whom they had never met and, on the other hand, the desire on the part of this Nazarene family to do something special for God and their church in return, contradict all those who insist that only selfish interests spur people to act in Africa.

Three months later, on a rainy morning with clouds hanging low over the city of Nairobi, missionary Harmon Schmelzenbach and I made our way to Wilson Airport. This airfield mainly serves general aviation and is situated about 20 miles from Kenya's International Airport. Both of us being pilots, we felt a little uneasy about the weather conditions. After going through the departure formalities, we boarded the small six-seater airplane with an Austrian pilot. After a short takeoff run, we climbed to approximately 200 feet above ground to stay below the cloud ceiling. Our route took us over the red roofs of Africa Nazarene University. Its location at the edge of a great game park with Nairobi's skyline as a backdrop certainly was unique. Immediately thereafter, having crossed the river ravine, we saw herds of wildebeest, zebra, and giraffes. It was a beautiful morning in spite of the gloomy skies. It inspired us to thoughtfully acknowledge God's preeminence and guidance in the church's endeavors here in Africa.

After overflying the escarpment to the south, the ground dropped away, giving us more height while staying at the same altitude. The scenery became exhilarating. As we flew toward Tanzania, we admired the majesty of "old man" Kilamanjaro, Africa's highest mountain, on our left. And to our right, almost underneath, we gazed in awe at the Ngorongoro Crater, a wildlife paradise where lions sleep in trees. Then the desolate Serengeti, vast as a mighty sea, captivating and fascinating.

We reached Dodoma in Tanzania after just over two

hours. Immigration procedures slow as ever, then changing in-to a small C-185 trail-dragger, we took off again, this time heading toward Mbeya, a town just north of Lake Malawi and just east of the Zambian border.

My thoughts went back to the beginning of all this. How marvelously God had led and how real His guiding presence had been!

We expected Rev. George Kaputula and possibly others from the Zambia North District to be in Mbeya to introduce us to the people with whom they had contact and whom we had set out to visit. It had been very difficult, almost impossible, to contact any of the people ahead of time to coordinate our trip. So we had decided to take whatever would come and be happy with whatever we would find on arrival. We hoped that our Zambian Nazarenes would track us down somehow. This was not the first time for such a venture.

Two hours later we approached the little dusty landing strip of Mbeya. After a bumpy landing, we taxied to the parking area. Suddenly we noticed an old, beat-up yellow truck from which several people were getting out. We disembarked and were stretching after the not-too-comfortable plane ride when five people from the truck ran toward us. We recognized our friends: Zambia North District Superintendent George Kaputula; Paul Katonga, one of the four Zambian Nazarene elders; Shadrack Simbeye, Lunde's father; and Jameson Mwanasepe, a strong Nazarene layman from Shadrack's church. They in turn introduced the brother who was the leader of the Tanzanian group, standing a little to one side.

After the welcome, introductions, and greetings, I asked Rev. Kaputula how they had come to the airfield since they had expected us to come by car. His reply: "We had an urge to come to the airfield. We were wondering if you would possibly come by plane since we knew you do a lot of flying."

All of us stood in amazement and then had a prayer of thanksgiving. Once more we realized that God had been down the road before us and had His hand in all of this. Another miracle!

It was early Saturday afternoon. Rev. Andambike wanted us to visit certain churches at Lake Malawi, including the biggest congregation of his group, approximately 80 miles southwest. I asked—I should have known better after my many years in Africa—how far these places would be. "Not too far" was the innocent answer—ouch!

What a ride! Hour upon hour over rough terrain. Potholes that seemed almost big enough to swallow a one-ton load of sand or bricks. Banana "forests" interspersed with coffee and tea fields. Narrow roads and mudslides in the steep mountains, dense bush in the valleys. A kaleidoscope of color and impressions.

It was dark by the time we came into the vicinity of our destination. How much farther? "Just across the river and around the bend." Eventually, however, we came to the river and found that the bridge had been washed away. No chance to get across—we stood on the shore and pondered.

Being already in the extended flood areas of great Lake Malawi, Brother Andambike and one of his pastors decided to lead us on a shortcut to a ford where we might be able to traverse the water. That "shortcut" became longer and longer and the terrain progressively more soggy.

At nightfall we got stuck for the first time. People appeared virtually out of nowhere. They stood up to their knees and thighs in water and mud. They tried to be helpful, shoving and pushing in all directions. We did our best. Wheels spun, mud splashed, people screamed, and a million mosquitoes provided background music with their hum. It seemed useless, but we repeated the process several more times. Sadly, we were only about one mile from our destination but were forced to turn around and barely made it back onto solid ground. We returned to Mbeya in the early hours of the morning. What a day that had been!

Through all of these thrills, intimidating to some and exciting to others, the God-glorifying conclusion to all of them will remain an unforgettable and spiritual impression. Both Harmon and I felt tremendous gratitude when we looked at the commitment of a people who have so little in material goods yet offer so much in spiritual fortitude.

The night was short in regard to sleep time. It was now

Sunday. After the morning service in a banana-leaf church, we sat with the elders around a table in our Tanzanian brother's humble abode—a clay hut with grass roof, no windows, and only one door. Sitting there, sharing the food, enjoying the fellowship, we discussed the issues and sensed each other's spirit and godly fervor to do what the Lord would have us do. This room was a lounge, dining area, bedroom, and district office all in one. We searched for God's will for all of us, sensing that even the sometimes-not-altogether-pleasant experiences of the previous day had provided a common meeting ground and a degree of brotherhood that now enhanced our conversations.

As we spoke about the Church of the Nazarene and asked questions in reference to Bible principles and *Manual* stipulations, we found again and again that our Zambian Nazarenes had prepared the way—laying the stones, paving the road, plowing the ground, sowing the seed, and opening the door. The fruit was ripe.

We had a map of Tanzania before us. One by one we marked the churches, the congregations, and their members as we spoke about our new parish. They explained that there were many opportunities if we would be interested in helping to reach out. A pastor, we learned, would go from time to time on three-month trips by foot to visit congregations and outposts. Up the mountains he would climb, and down the embankments he would slide in order to preach, teach, and encourage.

We made plans to train these good-hearted but simple lay preachers for further service. We promised to provide them with good-quality literature. All they had were three simple, well-worn booklets on the things of God and church structure principles. This was the full extent of their library. We proposed a training program whereby these students would help in their free time to till fields, plant beans, harvest bananas, and sustain themselves without any pay in cash or hard money. Talk about dedication!

That afternoon, sheltered from the piercing African sun by a canopy of grass, we bonded and pledged and committed to take into the Church of the Nazarene these congregations. It was a small but solid beginning.

We sealed this agreement with a song and a prayer as we formed a circle around the map of Tanzania, holding hands and asking God's blessings.

The people did not ask for any money. In fact, they told us that Rev. Kaputula on his trips had informed them that the Church of the Nazarene is not an organization given to "buying" people or congregations. Their motivation for wanting to join the great Nazarene movement was to be a part of a world denomination having the same goals, being driven by the same urgency, and sharing the same burdens, winning a lost world to Jesus.

As we made our way back to Kenya, flying over the savannah of western Tanzania, we reflected on our remarkable visit there. It had all started with a little crippled boy to whom people in the church had shown compassion by providing a way for relief and healing.

Update: Today in Tanzania we enjoy the faithful labor of almost 4,000 Nazarenes in two districts with 50 churches and 93 preaching points. Regional missionary Rev. Wellington Obotte of Kenya serves as mission coordinator for the entire country.

5
The Preacher Boy of Queru

Liberation is not an automatic grant to freedom.
To be liberated "from" is subjective — it has a tag.
You can be liberated from "this" and
be made captive to "that."
To be free is generic — it is all-encompassing.
Such freedom comes only from God.

Zimbabwe 1989. Rev. Enoch Litswele, mission director in this country, had invited me to be the keynote speaker in his forthcoming pastors' conference in Queru. I asked the regional coordinator for evangelism, Rev. Fred Huff, to be part of the program and to come with me.

The one-hour flight from Johannesburg to Bulawayo in the south of Zimbabwe went well. At the airport we rented a car and proceeded to drive the two and a half hours up into the high-lying areas of Queru. The time on the road would give us a good opportunity to talk and to share once more how we would plan the teaching ministry for our pastors in the conference.

First Event

After about one and a half hours, we suddenly heard a noise from underneath the car. We stopped to check it out but found nothing. We went on, only to hear the same noise again a few minutes later. This time I looked in the rearview mirror and saw what seemed to be a piece of tire catapulting across the road. We stopped again and checked but found no problems—the tires seemed to be all in order. Again we were on our way but had not gone far when the noise came back, this time like an explosion. The car started to skid from one side to the other, and I knew we had burst a tire. I was able to regain control and stopped at the roadside to change the tire. But we were unable to find the spare tire, nor did the car contain any tools.

We stood by the road and waited, hoping to wave down a passing driver. It wasn't long before a Peugeot 403 stopped. The driver, an elderly man, got out and asked if there was anything he could do to help us. We explained our predicament. "Let's try my tools and see if my spare wheel will fit," he said. The tools were just right. We took the wheel off and found the cause of our dilemma—chunks as big as a man's fist had been torn out on the inside of the tire. That's why we didn't find the problem earlier. The rest of the tire was nothing but burned, shredded rubber.

Miraculously, with a little knocking and bending, we were able to force our friend's spare wheel onto the axle, although it was a little smaller than ours. I turned to Fred and said, "This is Africa. In your and my countries we would probably not find a car rental company as careless as the one in Bulawayo—but we would also have to look very hard to find such friendly, unselfish help."

Slowly we drove the 25 kilometers to the next town. There we were able to purchase a used tire at quite an expense—no new ones could be found. We gave our "Good Samaritan" friend a sufficient gift of Zimbabwe dollars for his kindness and his trouble, and off we went with a very expensive used tire on the original wheel and eventually arrived at the conference in Queru.

Second Event

Queru was high up in the hills, and since it was midyear—winter in the Southern Hemisphere—it was very cold. Fred and I moved into one of the little rooms and at first look knew that this would be a cold stay. Our two mattresses had only one blanket each, and there was no fireplace.

Despite the cold, our reception was very warm. Rev. Litswele and the pastors from the two Zimbabwe districts welcomed us so heartily that we felt good from the very start. Our upset spirits at the car rental company that allowed us to drive up-country with a damaged tire, with no spare wheel and no tools, soon faded away.

We learned then of a special agenda item for the conference. Rev. Leah Mthembu, the only female pastor in Zimbabwe, had invited her uncle, who happened to be one of Zimbabwe's cabinet ministers. She knew Mr. Ushewakunze from before she was a Christian when they were together, he an officer in the Liberation Army and she one of the "camp girls" serving that army. Together with many others, they were part of the guerilla forces fighting the Rhodesian army from across the border in Mozambique. After independence, Mr. Ushewakunze had become minister for water affairs and energy in the new government. It was he who was scheduled to come and address the Nazarene pastors at Queru.

The pastors, of course, were very excited to have their church so recognized. Never before had a cabinet minister come all the way from Harare to speak to them.

On the second day of our conference, during the second session, a great commotion took place outside. As is the case in many African countries, an important politician would make his entry with great show and much noise. So it was here at Queru. Two cars loaded with rifle-carrying bodyguards, blue lights, and headlamps flashing spearheaded the way for the third car, out of which the minister alighted. We stopped our program and went outside to welcome our famed guest.

I then had the opportunity to take him into what was our very humble abode with the two mattresses on which Fred and I had made our beds for the night. We sat down on an old sofa whose most outstanding attribute was the big holes that covered it. A little embarrassed, I apologized for the simple reception. Mr. Ushewakunze understood. He smiled and very warmly mentioned that he knew he was not in the president's mansion and that he would not expect anything else. "My country is poor, and the warmth of your reception makes up for the thrifty room." With African politeness, he continued and said, a twinkle in his eye, "If it's good enough for white visitors from South Africa, it's good enough for me."

"This man really knew how to make an impression, create a relaxing atmosphere, and win friends," I thought.

We introduced him to the program and asked him how long he would want to speak. He requested an hour, and we went over to the meeting hall.

As we entered, all of our pastors stood and greeted the minister with great applause. We then witnessed a momentous spectacle. That's about the best way to describe what happened.

The bodyguards in shining uniforms, rifles not over their shoulders but in their hands, as if expecting an enemy attack at any moment, manned every window and entrance. The minister walked to the front of the hall and politely addressed the Church of the Nazarene as represented by the pastors. He was tall and slim and very well dressed. His dignified and yet exuberant personality created an atmosphere of awe, and that was matched by an eloquence that would have graced any preacher.

I've always said that Africans are born orators. When they get going, they really get going. Mr. Ushewakunze was a prime example of that. We had a blend of storyteller, magician, and entertainer all in one person. He drove home his points, always careful to balance tears of shame with tears of joy. He had no notes. He had no lectern or pulpit—he paced from one side of the room to the other and had everyone in the hall spellbound. Our guest related stories of how the freedom fighters resisting the Rhodesian army in the war of independence hid in the bush and how they used witchcraft to alert them of the enemy.

Of course, he was touching some very sensitive strings in the hearts of our pastors who emotionally would also feel proguerilla, proindependence, and pro-Zimbabwe government. That was fine with me. However, the point that Mr. Ushewakunze made skillfully and empathically was that Africa is Africa, that witchcraft had its place, being anchored in the sacred traditions and cultures of this continent.

What was he after? He was speaking to Holiness preachers, and he knew it. What did he have in mind? Where did he want to go? I became increasingly uncomfortable and noticed that Rev. Enoch Litswele, an African, a strong Nazarene church leader from South Africa and now mission director in Zimbabwe, was also becoming rather restless.

As our guest came to the close of his hour-long speech, he illustrated by sharing that his mother was a "born-again Christian," emphasizing that this was her term. But he ridiculed the expression. Using rather cynical formulations, he related how she had tried again and again to turn him to the Bible. "Storyteller," he called her, saying that the Bible was the comfort of an old woman.

He was by no means disrespectful to his mother, but he tried to make his point that she, like many others in Africa, had been "poisoned" by early missionaries who had come in days gone by to exploit Africa, using the Christian religion to enslave and subdue the people of this continent.

By now I was very upset. We were guests in this man's country. He was a cabinet minister. He addressed Zimbabwe nationals, and it was only about 10 years after the country had attained independence. Feelings of patriotism and nationalism and feelings against white people were still strong. On top of it all, he displayed so much charm and so much warmth while he spoke that no one could accuse him of being acrimonious or downright nasty. As I said, he was a master orator.

It became a very uncomfortable situation. There I was, the regional director of the Church of the Nazarene on the African continent. These were our pastors, Nazarene preachers, who were being addressed. I was white, a foreigner, a guest of the country. And yet I could not let this go by. If I did not say anything, I would have made myself guilty of denial, like Peter on the night when he betrayed Jesus. Silence would be speaking loudly, saying, "I do not know this man called Jesus."

Mr. Ushewakunze's speech finally came to an end. He thanked Rev. Leah, whom he praised as someone also completely committed and dedicated to the liberation of the country, placing that above everything else. She was family for him, he said. Then he sat down.

I got up. Having learned the African way, I suppressed my European way of handling a situation of this kind. Politely I thanked Mr. Ushewakunze for having taken the time to come all the way from Harare to address the pastors of the Church of the Nazarene. I expressed appreciation for the nice and charming way in which he did it, but then I said the following:

"Your Excellency, just as Paul before King Agrippa [Acts 25—26], I would respectfully want to explain to you aspects of which you seem to be unaware. Missionaries from across the seas had not come to exploit Africa. We do not deny that there may have been individuals with excesses, but on the whole, they came to bring the good news of a Savior, our Lord Jesus Christ, who gave himself for the redemption of humanity. Not all who have white faces know Him or follow Him, and not all who have black faces have really understood what He was all about.

"Mr. Minister, we are not here to tamper with African culture, nor do we plan to destroy African tradition. But just as my people in Germany without God walk in darkness, having no hope for tomorrow, so the people of Africa have the right to see the light and enjoy the privileges of the freedom, the peace, and the love that only Jesus Christ can bring.

"Your Excellency, allow me to suggest that it would have been better, considering the level of your education and the wisdom derived from your experiences, had you listened to your mother. As you described her, she must have been a sweet lady, a dignified *gogo* of an African family with a yearning to have her children find what she had found, that is, life and fulfillment not only for here on earth but also for eternity through her Lord and Savior, Jesus Christ.

"Thank you again for your efforts, and may you have a good journey back to Harare. I would like to present you with a gift, and I trust you will accept it. If ever there is a moment or an hour in which you feel that you are alone, that nobody understands you, or if ever there is doubt in your mind regarding the direction your life has taken, please read this book. It is the Word of God that we call the Holy Bible. I assure you that you will find comfort, encouragement, and peace for your soul."

With these words I presented a Bible to him. He smiled, thanked me, and said that he would accept it in the spirit in which it was given.

At that moment Rev. Litswele stood up. What would he say? Well, we saw a demonstration of Christian truth poured into the mold of pure African diplomacy. Rev. Litswele opened the Bible and addressed the minister in this way: "Your Excellency, Mr. Ushewakunze, minister of water affairs for Zimbabwe, we thank you for coming and speaking to us. You have been entrusted with the responsibility to secure and manage the water reserves for the country [water being the most precious commodity in Africa]. Permit me to introduce you to another minister of water affairs" [and then he read from John 7:38: "'Whoever believes in me, as the Scripture has said, streams of living water will flow from within him.'

"You see, Sir, as we follow Him, we will always have abundant supply. All of us here feel honored by your presence. You are a 'big man,' and you have taken time to visit us. Having introduced you to this Heavenly Minister of water affairs, we would humbly ask you to fall in step with Him. God bless you—we all wish you well."

After that he sat down. Mr. Ushewakunze acknowledged briefly and courteously and left the hall, walking past his bodyguards, who followed behind him. After the slamming of doors and the screeching of tires, the little convoy was gone.

What a day! That night, Fred and I remarked how beautifully and graciously Rev. Litswele found the right words before his men, dismantling any evil that might otherwise have lingered on or developed.

Third Event

The next morning I was to leave. Fred would stay behind for the rest of the conference. I wanted to make my way back to catch the plane to Johannesburg.

It was early in the morning with winter temperatures up in the mountains close to the freezing point when I drove out of our camp onto the main road. I had not gone very far in the direction of Bulawayo when I saw a young man standing with his bag at the side of the road. He thumbed a lift. While it is normally not advisable in Africa to pick up hitchhikers, I felt that early on a cold morning like this, such a young man would not have any bad intentions. I stopped and told him that I was on my way to Bulawayo. He said that this was where he wanted to go also. He put his bag on the backseat and stepped in.

I was just about to start up the car again when the young man reached over to me and said, "Sir, would you mind if I just thanked God?"

"This is really something else," I thought. We folded our hands and he prayed, "Thank You, God, for answering my petition in sending this driver for me as I had asked You to. Help him drive safely. Bless us and give us a good journey to Bulwayo."

I then said to the young man, "I hear you asked God to provide you transportation."

"Yes," he said, "and God answered my prayer within five minutes."

"I feel great, young man, and it's wonderful to know that I'm the answer to your prayer".

"God has many angels," he answered. I chuckled to myself. To the best of my memory, that was the first time I was ever identified as an angel.

"I take it you're a Christian," I said.

"Oh, yes," he said. "I come from the Baptist Bible School, which is just a little way up the road from the conference camp. I'm in my third year."

I learned that his name was Joseph and that he was born and grew up in a little village on the western side of Zimbabwe. He felt a call to preach and was now preparing for the ministry.

"Joseph, we have over two hours before us. I'm curious to find out how you became a Christian. Will you tell me the story?" I still had not told him who I was nor that I was a Christian.

"Oh, yes," he said. "It was like this." And what a beautiful testimony he shared!

Joseph's village consisted of about 300 people. Early in his life he, like all the other boys in the clan, was taught how to herd cattle. He spent day after day in the pastures, at the same time learning how to carve little figures from dried wood, to fight with sticks, and to differentiate between the various plants and trees.

Then came the time of schooling. There was a little church in the village made of bamboo poles and a reed roof. Pastor Simon was an old man, but he took his ministry very seriously. Everybody in the village knew him and loved him. It was also Pastor Simon who taught Joseph and the other boys how to read and write. The public school was very far away, and they would have to become a little older to walk there every day.

Joseph really did not go to church. Pastor Simon had been to his family's kraal on a number of occasions, but neither Joseph's mother nor his father were believers—in fact, his father was the brother of the village witchdoctor. They liked the pastor, but they would not go to church.

One day Pastor Simon approached Joseph and said, "Joseph, we're going to have a special play for the people of our village, and all the boys and girls will become actors and participate. Do you want to be part of it?"

He agreed, and his parents allowed him go to church for practice with the other children.

Days of practice went by in which Pastor Simon taught the Bible story to these young actors. Joseph, too, learned much through participating in every session.

The play was to portray Abraham and his son Isaac and how God would ask the father to sacrifice his son as proof of his devotion to God.

Joseph had wondered about that. This God would have to be a very special one—much more special than the "ghost gods" of which the witchdoctor uncle always spoke when he came to visit. But how could God ask a father to sacrifice his son even if he was special?

The day of the play arrived. There was great excitement in the village that afternoon as Pastor Simon and his helpers prepared the village plaza for the event. When evening had come and fires were lit, the story unfolded. There was much audience participation with laughter and with expressions of surprise as Pastor Simon moderated the account.

All actors played their role very well. But then it was Joseph's turn. His role was to play Isaac, the son of Abraham. He had to follow his father up a stack of wood that represented the mountain. Slowly Abraham and his servants, who carried the wood, and Isaac at the hand of his father, leading a goat (representing the donkey in the Gen. 22 account) came out of the dark and approached the mountain. "Stay there and keep the donkey," Abraham said to the servants. "My son and I will go up this mountain to worship and then come back to you."

Abraham then took the wood for the burnt offering and placed it on his son Isaac. He himself carried the firebrand and the knife. They stopped at the bottom of the mountain, and the father turned to his son and said, "My son, we are going up this mountain now to meet with our God. He loves us more than I could love you or you could love me. You will now have to trust your father in all he does, just as your father will have to trust God."

Isaac nodded in agreement, and together they slowly made their way up the wooden stack—the mountain.

As Joseph continued to relay the story to me, I noticed that he was emotionally stirred. He said, "You see, Sir, what followed was just out of the Word of God. I had to say, 'Father,' and Abraham replied, 'Yes, my son.'

"'I see the fire and the wood, Father, but where is the lamb for the burnt offering?'

"Abraham answered, 'God himself will provide the lamb, my son,' and up we went." With wet eyes, Joseph turned to me while I tried to keep my eyes fixed on the road. He explained, "You see, Sir, in that moment it seemed as if God were speaking to me. He was saying, 'I have provided the burnt offering—the sacrifice is for you. All you need to do is to accept and to follow me.'

"I knew at that moment that this whole play was for me. God came into my heart there and then. I broke out in tears. I knew I was unworthy. How could I let God down, who had provided? Who was I to reject what He gave of His own? This is how I became a Christian."

We were silent for a few moments. I was deeply moved. The impact of this young man's testimony struck cords deep down in my heart. He had preached a powerful message by simply recalling how he became a Christian.

It was then that I told him who I was and that really we were brothers. He rejoiced. "I knew it!" he exclaimed. "I knew there was something special about you when I stepped into your car!"

We still had wonderful exchanges until we arrived at the airport. Before I returned the car to the company, lodging a complaint about tire situation, we paused for prayer. I gave my business card to Joseph and told him that if he should ever feel led to do so, he could call the missionary in Harare or the district superintendent.

Update: It was only a year later that I learned that Joseph had done so and that he had accepted the pastorate of a little church close to Plumtree at the border of Botswana.

"The preacher boy of Queru" and his testimony will forever be a strong motivator for me to testify of God's grace.

6
Night Hunt
in Kisumu

A cheerful heart is good medicine,
but a crushed spirit dries up the bones.
—Prov. 17:22

Kenya has its very own fascinating features. It's not by accident that this country is the most visited on the African continent. Planeload after planeload of tourists arrive in all seasons and from everywhere in the world to view East Africa's last phenomenal herds of game. Indeed, nothing on earth can compete with these huge numbers of wildebeest (gnu) and zebra in the Masai Mara during the time of migration. Exhilarating. Exhausting. Exciting! Numbers exceeding 1 million are not unusual, and the spectacle of the Serengeti in motion, movement as far as the eye can see, is one never to be forgotten.

I had an encounter in 1986 that also left an indelible impression on me, though completely different. The night was sultry and humid in Kisumu, in western Kenya, as Harmon and Beverly Schmelzenbach and I pulled into the hotel parking place at the east shore of Lake Victoria. It had been a beautiful but tiring day visiting outlying areas. The old four-wheel drive Patrol had served us well. Its shock absorbers must have been worn to the hilt, however.

There had been no highways, no tar roads, not even gravel roads that day. In fact, some of the deep gullies had to be carefully circumnavigated—the potholes had become pot *pools.* Entire cars could have disappeared in them. My back felt as if it had served as front and rear suspension all day. When we eventually got to our rooms, we were ready for the bed and a restful night.

Our evening meal was brief, and our conversation consisted of a few reflections of the day, which served only to make us even more tired. By consensus, we decided to have a shower in the morning rather than at night.

A final good-night to each other, a very brief prayer to the Lord, and getting completely undressed (there was no air conditioning), I fell into bed and was half asleep five minutes later. My missionary companions, Harmon and Beverly Schmelzenbach, had the room next door.

But then, was it dream or reality? Something moved in the room, and it wasn't me. My senses began to work again, rather sluggishly at first, but increasingly functional. There it was again!

By now I was sure that I wasn't dreaming. Could it be a mouse? No, it was too loud for that. A rat, perhaps? It would not have been the first time. I listened into the dark, trying to pinpoint the direction. There it was again. The noise came from the window. I decided to investigate, since I could not persuade myself to ignore it. All kinds of thoughts went through my weary mind. Nighttime always intensifies one's imagination.

Slowly I rolled out of bed as my ears, like shortwave antennae, scanned the room. I turned the light on. Not that this dim 25-watt bulb hanging suspended on a wire from the ceiling helped very much. Cautiously I moved toward the curtain. The windows, I knew, were tightly shut to keep out mosquitoes, which are plentiful near the great lake.

There it was again! Very distinct, a scraping sound like claws against glass. Ready for anything, I took a shoe in one hand and quickly jerked the curtain aside with the other hand—and out flew a bat. Yes, an ordinary bat. Only God knows how it got behind that curtain. But now the peace was gone. No more tranquillity as this animal started to circle around the room like a jet fighter. Its speed was phenomenal, its navigation even more so. Not once did it touch a wall.

10 P.M. I had to make a plan now. I could not open the window more than one foot. Would I ever be able to chase it out there? I would certainly try! Frantically I waved my shoe. I fanned my arms until they felt like lead—to no avail.

10:30 P.M. I had to make another plan. I closed the window and opened the door instead—as far as it was possible. The door led onto the prolonged open-air corridor from which one can look across the atrium to the opposite side of the building. I exchanged the shoe for a bath towel. The bigger weapon should make things easier.

11 P.M. I was still at it—by now rather exhausted with two towels, one in each hand. Would that bat never get tired? Not once had I hit it, and I had surely tried. All the time, however, I had been very noise-conscious, well realizing that I was by no means the only guest in the hotel. But suddenly as I did see one or two lights across the yard being turned on, I got the shock of my life: I had been parading in my creation safari suit! I was as naked as when I had been born. The sudden realization caused me to slam the door shut with a bang, and for the first time I heard rumblings in the rooms next to mine. The bat was still in circuit.

11:30 P.M. Tired, weary, red with embarrassment, panting like an old bullfrog, dizzy from all the turning and twisting, I decided on another plan of action. Surely, if I turned the light out, the bat would also prefer a complete stop and, hopefully, get some rest till morning.

12 midnight. Pulling the sheet over my perspiring, wet body, I turned out the light and tried to close my eyes. As I intensely tried turning my thoughts on something nice—my home, my wife, the supportive staff at the office—I inevitably found my thoughts returning to this creature in the dark. I heard mosquitoes humming—no, not mosquitoes. The noise was too loud. The hum was more like the flapping of air being blown through a comb, as we used to play as children. No, it was this East African dive-bomber, its radar scanning my room, continuing to practice aerobatics. I began to differentiate the sound as it approached from the sound when it left after its flyby. It was a bit like being in the grandstand during an air show. Did somebody not tell me that bats go for the hair of a person and that once it arrived it would not come out?

12:30 A.M. Now, I didn't have all that much hair left on my head, but there was still too much to allow this creature to create havoc. And imagine having to get a bat out of one's hair in the middle of the night.

I pulled the sheet up over my head. But try to stay there with a 95° temperature and not a breeze of air. I don't know how long I was down there. It was just like holding your breath underwater—you have to come up once in a while for air.

1 A.M. I could not stand it any longer. Every time the "enemy" approached, I would go for cover: down and up, down and up—what was I to do? We were to leave at daybreak around 4 A.M., and I hadn't had a wink of sleep.

1:30 A.M. I finally decided on a scheme of total annihilation. I had had enough. My patience had run dry, and out of the bed I hopped. I turned my 25-watt electric globe on again and prepared for battle. This time it was going to be "nuclear war." No longer just a shoe or a towel. No, I planned to throw my full firing power at the enemy: ground-to-air missiles. I opened my suitcase. Painstakingly I took out some shirts and socks and pants. I carefully weaved them into giant balls. I took the towels and wrapped my shoes in them. Two of my ties helped to "wire" these deadly charges. I then took the sheets off my bed, folding them fourfold so as to have wide-area coverage. I planned to use them together with the blankets like World War II interception balloons to trap enemy aircraft.

2 A.M. I was ready for the final showdown. Carefully I arranged my armament on the bed now totally depleted of sheets while the enemy was still circling overhead, unperturbed by my offensive preparations. Then I went into action. No question: this was Agent 007 at his best. I waited for another approach, having had plenty of time during the last few hours to study the pattern. I hurled missile after missile. Shoes flying, towel grenades exploding, pillowcases filled with newspaper ripped the air. The enemy tried to dodge them, at first very successfully, but then it seemed to be slowing down. Probably low on fuel, I mused. I decided on the final barrage. The blankets and the folded sheets went into action, and one of them indeed made contact. The bat was finally on the ground, still moving, though, and attempting another takeoff, but a well-aimed cosmetic bag connected and blew its lights out.

2:30 A.M. It all seemed so unreal. The silence, so loud that it almost hurt. My blood throbbing. My pulse racing. My head still spinning. The room a picture of devastation. I began to gather some of the items. I collected the bat and transferred it out into the corridor. Exhausted, I sank onto my bed, and the last time I looked at the clock it was 2:45 A.M.

The alarm went off at 4 A.M. My limbs heavy as lead, I drug myself to the bathroom and took a cold shower. I wanted to have my morning devotions, but ironically, only one verse seemed to enter my mind: *You have fought a good fight.* I wondered as I tried to pray whether that was for me or for my foe!

As we packed our car early next morning, fresh air blowing from the lake, Harmon and Beverly wondered what all the noise was about during the night. They were so tired that they did not get up to investigate.

I eventually confessed. As we drove to Homa Bay Church for a dedication service, we all had a good laugh. My laugh, I'm sure, was a little weak and tired. Indeed, church work in Africa can be exhilarating and sometimes also a "bit" tiring.

7
They Labored Not in Vain

The growth of the church today is rooted in a century of faith and hard work by committed servants of the Lord.

*T*rimming our single-engine Cessna 206 aircraft for descent, we broke cloud. I handed the controls back to Gene Patrick,* who took over for landing. Early in the morning we had taken off in Chimoio, somewhere in the center of Mozambique. A great dedication service in the new church there, with following celebration, had taken us late into the night on the previous day. Our flight this Sunday morning was routing from Chimoio to the extreme north of that great country. Furancungu, venue of the first Nazarene mission settlements in that part of the world many years ago, was our destination.

I had enjoyed flying the plane. Now, as I looked down at the passing landscape, beholding the great African bush and the mountains, my mind raced. My heart filled with anticipation and excitement—what would we find? Missionary Theodore Esselstyn's words from a few days before, when I told him of this trip, were still ringing in my ears: "That's the end of the world. . . . My father took me there in 1955, crossing rivers and scaling boulders. . . . It took us 17 hours for the last 90 miles."

*Gene Patrick, friend and colaborer, died in a small plane crash in the United States during 1999.

Thank God for Nazarene aviation in Africa. How much simpler, how much less complicated, how much easier we have it today, just flying in! Looking down and following the winding road, seeing the little outpost of Cazula pass by, I was reminded that the long and cruel civil war in Mozambique reached its most horrific peak precisely in this area. I wondered what we would find.

We knew from our district superintendent, Matias Beta, that no people had been living in that area for many years. The last missionaries, Oscar and Marjorie Stockwell, left in 1970. In her book about her husband, *The Lord's Boy*, Marjorie recalled the circumstances of their departure. The war zone had approached, and these heroic missionaries stayed to the very last. They barely made their way out. Attacks became more frequent. Travel was possible only in convoys. Exploding land mines, planted at night on the roads, accounted for burned-out vehicles, the many mutilated bodies, and the numerous fatalities. It seemed to be the end of Nazarene missions in that part of the world.

After the last missionaries had left, the fortunes of war changed back and forth, sometimes favoring the left and sometimes the right. Continued attacks, man-to-man fighting, mortar shells, and hand grenades destroyed two beautiful mission homes, a Bible college, a clinic, and a school. It seemed that this chapter in the church's history had indeed closed in this country.

After the last people had fled the horrors of the war, Mozambican Nazarenes found themselves as refugees as far away as Zambia and Malawi. The bush took over the country again, and by 1980, 10 years later, hardly a wall could be spotted. Primeval vegetation had swallowed the mission station as well as the surrounding villages. Apart from sporadic appearances of soldiers from both sides, the area became as it must have been 200 years ago.

As Gene circled to check out the airstrip and the wind direction, my thoughts went to these Nazarene refugees, many of whom I had met during the last 10 years in either Dedza, Malawi, or Ukwimi, Zambia. I would like to share two unforgettable experiences that demonstrate God's marvelous ways.

Zambia—February 1992. Missionary Lowell Clark in Lusaka, Zambia, had told me about these refugees from across the border from Mozambique. They were given land in the wilderness of Zambia, about 500 miles east of Lusaka in an area called Ukwimi. He reported that a delegation of Nazarenes from this refugee settlement had appeared in Lusaka, having walked all this way to request permission from the South District in Zambia to organize churches in the Ukwimi area. Brother Clark went on to tell me that he made a visit there and said how impressed he was to find such motivated, energetic, and faithful Nazarenes during his visit there. After some time, he received word that they were ready to dedicate their first church building and asked if I would be able to put a service into my schedule.

Would I come? What a question! I knew of the suffering of these people. I was aware of their plight. Finding themselves in a strange land, having received permission from the district to organize themselves, they had begun, seemingly undaunted, to establish the church. Now they were ready for the dedication of a new building.

We traveled the dusty road from Lusaka, almost a day's journey. When we arrived in the late afternoon, hundreds of people lined the path up through the high grass, waving branches in their hands, chanting, dancing, and singing praises to God.

What an evening we had! We rigged a sheet-screen, turned on a generator, and showed the *Jesus* film in that clear and moonless night. It was an exhilarating experience. Everywhere bodies. Movement all around in the darkness. Faces could be only faintly made out in the reflection of the light, which was beamed through the projector lens onto the screen. Oohs and ahs, sounds of agreement or disgust, a chuckle here, a sob there, were the only interruptions. A final prayer, uttered by a thousand voices, concluded a glorious evening.

The next day, Sunday morning, we entered the newly constructed church, crudely constructed with rocks that the women had carried in traditional style on their heads from a quarry eight miles away. It stood as though it had been built to last at least a hundred years. Rafters consisting of branches from the bush, tied together with plaited strings made from dried cornstalks, held the roof. Four small windows—no frame and no glass, just openings the size of my briefcase with a wooden cross in the middle—provided the scant ventilation in the building.

And then the service—with 952 people in attendance. How do I know the exact number? Mozambicans have a unique system. They had taken 1,000 corn kernels, and each person entering the church received 1—48 were left. It was a full sanctuary. All 952 people were cramped into this building with temperatures in the upper 90s. Others crowded around the outside, peeping in through the window openings and by doing so strangling the airflow to the inside.

What do you preach to a people who have gone through the worst kind of experiences? Some in my congregation were mutilated, with no arms or legs. Some had lost ears, lips, and noses, cut off by enemy soldiers. Others had witnessed the murder of their loved ones through torture and other brutalities. Some had lost loved ones to wild animals, to crocodiles in the river, or to lions in the bush as they fled the terrors of war.

I selected Ps. 23 as my text. "The Lord is my Shepherd"— yes, there are the green pastures, the quiet waters, the paths of righteousness, I said. Yes, there is restoration of the soul—but sometimes we're not spared the walk through the valley of the shadow of death. These committed people had been there—in more ways than one.

The meal afterward was a great time of sharing. The only goat in the camp had been slaughtered for the visitors. The liver, wrapped neatly in intestines and strips of stomach, a specialty in that part of the world, was served with love and joy.

When we parted, someone in our party asked if there was anything we could do for them. Listen to Mr. Phiri's (the leading layman's) reply, "Continue to pray for us, for our land, for our people, for those who have been left behind, and, if it's possible, let us have some salt."

What humble requests! What frugal petitions! Yes, we had tasted the food. It was delicious, but it contained no added salt. Going home, we decided that through our Compassionate Ministry program we would get them salt, and they got it—enough!

I left Ukwimi a stronger Christian, a more humble servant of my Lord. Truly, I received more than I was able to give.

Dedza, Malawi—March 1988. I was on the road from Blantyre to Lilongwe in Malawi. Between Ncheu and Dedza, for approximately 65 miles, the road serves as the border between Malawi and Mozambique. There's no border fence, no border post. Driving north, one passes the burned-out shacks and stalls that used to be operated in former days by Mozambicans who offered their goods to travelers passing by. Portuguese writings on some of the buildings can still be seen.

That's on the left side of the road. On the right side, new grass hut settlements have sprung up, almost the entire 65 miles. These dwellings are small, not more than six feet high, and house refugees who flooded in from across the road, from Mozambique.

As we were traveling, a commotion just ahead of us suddenly attracted our attention. A group of approximately 20 men, some of them bleeding, others bandaged, all of them in rags but carrying assault rifles, ran across the street. We stopped the car when we heard shots being fired and hit the ground for cover. We realized that yet others were in pursuit of those who had scrambled in front of us. However, they stopped short of following into Malawi, probably because other soldiers were nearby.

After the shooting had stopped, we waited awhile to make sure it was safe. Then we inquired as to whether we could help. People who had hidden in their grass huts during the incident came out. A man who identified himself as a pastor said that there was a first-aid station farther on and that he would take care of the wounded. Talking to him, I found out that he was a Nazarene and that numerous other Nazarenes were in that settlement as well. We left the wounded in their care.

What a shame that this continent continued to be

plagued by unrest, bloodshed, and war. How shocking to come face-to-face with it, a brief rendezvous with African reality in 1988.

Two years later, in May 1990, I received a letter at the regional office written in broken English:

Dear Doctor:

I have just read in the latest issue of the *Trans-African* [the Church of the Nazarene magazine for Africa], that our church needs pastors for Nazarene people in Mozambique. God spoke to me. . . . I feel guilty, having left. I will sacrifice myself. When you receive this letter . . . I will be back in Mozambique. . . . I will search for our people who remained. Please pray for me. . . . I am throwing myself into the arms of Jesus on the foundation of Philippians 1:20-21.

Yours,
Rev. Bonga Laitane

At that time the war was still raging, with people still fleeing the country when they could. I immediately opened my Bible. My eyes filled with tears when I read the verses Rev. Laitane had referred to: "I eagerly expect and hope that I will in no way be ashamed, but will have sufficient courage so that now as always Christ will be exalted in my body, whether by life or by death. For to me, to live is Christ and to die is gain" (Phil. 1:20-21).

Above this verse in my Bible I wrote, "Rev. Bonga Laitane returned to Mozambique—May 16, 1990." Was this not the Pastor Bonga whom I met two years before on the road to Dedza when these soldiers crossed?

For years thereafter I did not hear from him. Year after year, I wondered if he was still alive, regularly uplifting him to our Lord. Was he glorifying God as a preacher back in his country, or had he perhaps already entered heaven as a martyr?

Philippians is my favorite book in the New Testament. I have preached more sermons from this letter than from any other book in the Bible. So every time I read from it, I would see my note at 1:20-21.

Indeed, Brother Laitane's faithfulness, courage, and desire to do the will of God became another great incentive for me in my work. New motivation for my ministry and for my life as regional director for the church in Africa was born.

Furancungu—August 20, 1995. We were now on final approach to the overgrown runway, surrounded by mountains and wild terrain. A group of people next to a large orange truck on the ground looked up at us. A lone eagle catching an updraft on our right broke the monotony of the picture.

Gene landed the plane, taxied over the bumpy field, and came to a halt. As we left the plane, we were greeted with great singing in Portuguese and Chichewa by the "welcome committee." District superintendent Matias Beta and his wife led the group, each person waving a palm branch and singing, "God is so good, / God is so good, / God is so good, / He's so good to me!" We recognized the words by the tune.

Two men came running toward me, stretching out their hands. I was startled. The first one asked, "Do you still remember me from Ukwimi in Zambia?" There he was—Mr. Phiri, whom I had met in Ukwimi, Zambia, the one who had led his people out of the war zone, who built the first refugee church, which I dedicated in 1992. How could I forget?

And then the other: "I am Bonga Laitane. I met you that day in Dedza and later wrote to you that I would return to Mozambique." I began to choke on my tears. With trembling hands I took my Bible out, opened it to Phil. 1:20-21, and showed him his name and the date on the page—May 16, 1990. He put his arms around me, and both of us sobbed. What a glorious, heavenly experience!

These good people all had come in that one truck—72 of them. By that time our other aircraft, coming from Beira with missionary Philip Troutman and field director Ken Walker, had also landed. All of them squeezed onto the open truck, while I had the privilege of sitting in the cabin. I had to smile at the thought that this was one time I was glad not to have a general superintendent with me—I would have also had to stand on the back of an open truck squeezed in with 72 other passengers!

Rev. Beta told us that we would first of all visit the *ru-*

inas. The 12-mile journey through the bush took about 30 minutes. More people and more joy as a few hundred more people gathered, followed, chanted, danced, smiled, sang, and welcomed.

What a sight! I'm not an emotional person, but I could hardly contain myself. We walked over to the ruins—and there I was introduced to another important part of Nazarene church history in Africa—not through books, not through lessons, not through sermons. I saw it firsthand. As we stood before these overgrown walls, Rev. Beta explained that this one had been Missionary Fairy Cochlin's house. I stepped into what used to be the living room and stood in front of the fireplace, grass all around me. No roof, no windows, no doors—only the shell of a once-beautiful home was left. I wondered how many times Sister Fairy had knelt before that fireplace and prayed. I was treading on holy ground.

Suddenly somebody touched me gently on the arm and warned me that land mines were still around and that I should not go any farther. The procession then went up a steep and bumpy hill. Under the moss we could see what used to be paving. The clinic, or what was left of it, was on the right-hand side. The church, with only a few walls still standing, reminded us that once upon a time there must have been a beautiful edifice on the left-hand side. Farther up, we saw another mission home. The Popes had lived there from 1934 to 1954. Other missionaries followed, the last ones being the Stockwells, who left in 1970.

Moving on, we saw the walls of the former Bible college, the old stone oven in the garden in which they baked their bread, a gravestone on the left—all in the midst of eight-foot-high elephant grass all around. Yet it seemed as if I was in an ivory palace. Never will I forget this moving experience.

From there I was guided down where a temporary grass shelter had been constructed to protect the preacher and guests from the burning sun. The congregation squatted before us on the ground, and the old church ruins provided the backdrop, completing the scene, for a memorable service. They began to sing. Small groups came forward—boys, girls, men, ladies. Rev. Beta, being hoarse from all the talking, praised God over and over again. The volume of singing increased from the quiet thank-you choruses to a crescendo of praise. We had 492 people in our congregation, again by exact count, this time through stick collection.

Then came my time to preach. My words were translated into Portuguese by Rev. Isaac Mandlate and from Portuguese into Chichewa by none other than my long-lost and now found friend, Rev. Bonga Laitane.

How did I ever make it through that service? I don't know. They told me that this was the first Nazarene church service at the mission station since 1970. Twenty-five long years of waiting, a generation in hope.

I scrapped the sermon I had prepared. I felt led to open the Word and read,

> Therefore, since we are surrounded by such a great cloud of witnesses, let us throw off everything that hinders . . . let us run with perseverance the race marked out for us. Let us fix our eyes on Jesus, the author and perfecter of our faith. . . . Remember your leaders, who spoke the word of God to you. Consider the outcome of their way of life and imitate their faith. Jesus Christ is the same yesterday and today and forever *(Heb. 12:1-2; 13:7-8)*.

Indeed, a cloud of witnesses surrounded us. A host of angels was with us, and God smiled upon His people. The stage had been prepared. The curtains opened. The heavenly orchestra was in tune—it was the nearest thing to heaven I had experienced.

Some of these old missionaries were still alive and among us at that time: Gladys Pope (who has since gone to heaven), Marjorie Stockwell, and "Old Man" Esselstyn. They, like us, had not yet completed the race. Others were with Jesus already, but all of them enjoy the dividends of their investment. Their sacrifice has been rewarded. Their labor has not been in vain.

More Beyond

Congregations are forming again in the area called Furancungu. I committed that day that with the help of God and faithful Nazarenes around the world, we would assist them in rebuilding the church. With preaching points springing up everywhere in the area, we will plan to have a new district in Furancungu during 1996.

It was only after my return to the regional office that I read the book *Into All the World,* by J. Fred Parker. He wrote that the first missionaries in Furancungu called the place "Plus Ultra"—"More Beyond." How true this has become!

After the service at the ruins, we prepared to feed these hundreds of people out there in the bush. Water had to be transported from far away, and only an old oil drum in which *nshima,* the traditional stiff corn meal porridge, had been cooked was available. A feast began. Groups of families sat here and there in the long grass. Some of us became a little fearful that at any moment one of them would step on one of the hidden land mines. A few meters away, a group of young-sters killed a cobra. Africa made itself known again, but God protected us all.

Before we left, a final ceremony took place. Mrs. Beta stepped forward and, with a speech of appreciation and grati-tude, presented me with a gavel. "This is for you to remember us by," she said. "We carved it out of the last wood from the roof rafters of the old mission home."

Then she gave me one for Mrs. Pope, for the children of Missionary Salmon, and for Mrs. Stockwell. How meaningful!

I was speechless, able only to utter thanks, promising to convey the gifts and the thoughts behind them. No, I'll never be the same again.

If I had one wish in all of it, it would be that I could take all of what is Nazarene to such heights of bliss. Never—I chuckle quietly at the thought—would the church have any problem raising sufficient money for the World Evangelism Fund and other offerings for missions again.

It was our privilege and joy to return to Furancungu one year later on July 29, 1996. This time I had Theodore Essel-styn with me, who, as previously stated, had made his first and only trip here as a teenager with his father in 1955. What a nostalgic journey it was for Brother Ted!

We had flown up from Manzini with Daniel Jones and Ken Walker, this time in our turbocharged C-210, somewhat faster than the old C-206 of the year before.

On the way up to Furancungu, on Saturday, we had a great dedication service for the newly constructed Bible college at Maputo. From there we flew to Xai-Xai on Sunday morning for a service. As we disembarked from our little plane, we were greeted by a teenage choir singing the "Hallelujah Chorus" from Handel's *Messiah*. I preached again to over 700 people in a church "skeleton" structure featuring reed mats and open skies.

From there we flew to Vilanculos, where we met Rev. Jonas Mulate, who was pioneering the church there. He greeted us at the airfield with these words: "This will be the first major service in the last province of Mozambique untouched by the Church of the Nazarene."

Rev. Mulate presented us with a list of goals: by the time of the 1997 General Assembly, he wanted to have 10 organized churches, 4 students in Maputo Bible College, training for the ministry, 10 lay ministers enrolled in the Education by Extension program, and 100 percent of his budgets paid. What an inspiration to be with such a forward thinker!

Finally we arrived in Furancungu, where again, as one year previously, we were greeted by a multitude of people, who led us singing and chanting to the newly built church.

Yes, we had been true to our word, and so had they. One year ago I had made the commitment that if they provided the labor, if they would clean the old clay bricks, scratch off the cement, make them reusable, and find the bricklayers, we would provide the funds to rebuild the church structure. And what a beautiful building it has become—appropriately built on the foundation of the former one.

Our hearts were touched and blessed as we looked into the congregation from the little platform in front. Approximately 650 people had crowded into a building with no pews and no chairs and sat on the floor like sardines in a can. Nobody could move backward or forward. Soloists and singing groups just had to stand where they were and present their specials.

When the offering plates were passed, no usher was able to get through—the plate was passed from person to person. People crowding outside around the church, unable to enter, threw their money through the airbricks in the walls, which serve as windows. They just rolled the bills together, threw them in, and, sure enough, people inside would catch the money in flight and put these precious rolls into the offering plate. Everybody wanted to participate.

About 20 meters from the church, the newly elected district superintendent had built his district parsonage: a crude grass hut with corner poles and clay walls, reinforced with reed and topped by a grass roof. It had no windows, just a little opening as a door. You have to bend down to enter. Rev. Thomas Phiri proudly showed us his self-made home.

As we left, blessed to the hilt, I made another commitment to the people: if they would supply labor, scratch the cement off any of the old clay brick they could find, and provide some bricklayers again, we would help them with some extra funds to rebuild the former home of missionary Fairy Cochlin to become the new district parsonage within the year. The people responded affirmatively, with cheering, singing, and praises to God.

Soon afterward, as we lifted off the little airfield and circled once more over the newly built church with the people waving up from the ground, the four of us rejoiced together.

Update: Today there are two districts and a total of 67 Nazarene churches in this area, making it a total of 32 districts and 50,000 Nazarenes in Mozambique. God has invested His Son, who gave His life. The dividends are uncountable. The church has invested—missionaries have gone and spent their lives for the Kingdom. Now all of us are privileged to invest in God's great work here and around the world. May we not fail in this great task. The promise of PLUS ULTRA—that there is MORE BEYOND—applies to all of us.

8

Who Catches a Buffalo with a Mosquito Net?

*Where God is in the center,
you will find genuine attempts
to be fair and just; you will find a philosophy of sharing
and a determination to improve this world—
and with Him you will succeed.*

Africa has a genius for extremes. Nowhere on earth is a day brighter or a night darker. Nowhere are forests more lush, deserts more barren and dry. Nowhere are natural resources in greater abundance, yet nowhere is poverty more striking.

Africa is a continent of uncounted mysteries with a trillion unanswered questions; a continent battered into submission by umpteen forces, desperately struggling to regain dignity and self-esteem.

A multiheaded monster of deforestation, urban overpopulation, disease, starvation, illiteracy, corruption, and social breakdowns stretches its ever-expanding tentacles, attempting to engulf and suffocate this continent. Vanishing resources, overcrowded cities, drought, war, and a deluge of refugees have swallowed billions of dollars since World War II, and yet its people have less today than 40 years ago. According to a

United Nations report about Africa, the agricultural produce of the continent was 20 percent less in 1990 than in 1955, yet feeding a population that had grown by 90 percent.

A multitude of workers in nongovernmental organizations are busy doing their thing. One finds these "do-gooders" just about anywhere on the continent. They sit in government offices, meet in hotel lobbies, and sip their coffee in airport lounges. Sometimes you find them in remote villages, often with little more than their rucksacks. Driven by idealism, supported by the results of extensive promotion campaigns in their home countries, these philanthropists have set out to change the world. It usually doesn't take too long, however, before frustration sets in and the stark reality in the face of seemingly ever-increasing calamities drives them to resignation. They then quickly relocate to more promising harvest fields in another part of the world. As suddenly as they come, they seem to disappear. Only very few dig in, get established, and do more than just provide an extra drop in the ever-expanding "bucket" of Africa's reality.

Don't try to catch a buffalo with a mosquito net. It indeed takes more than idealism, more than the proverbial greenback or a good portion of altruism to bring about change.

I had just landed in Addis Ababa, the capital city of Ethiopia. The aftermath of revolution, the resulting civil war, the ensuing massacres, and the almost two decades of Communist rule had left indelible scars. The drab appearance of the city, the dysfunctional sewerage systems during the many days of pouring rain were matched only by the plight of its people.

Human suffering accentuated by rapid urbanization with thousands flocking to the city from the arid rural areas of the country was reflected by the many street children and street families, all of whom seemed to have made Addis Ababa's inner city their abode. They're found pushed into doorways, pressed against walls, covered with soggy newspapers at night. They use just about any imaginable item to find shelter from the pouring rain.

I took a cab from the airport to my hotel. My driver, seemingly very happy that he had found a customer that morning,
put my suitcase into the car trunk and tied the lid of the trunk
to the bumper with a piece of string (the lock was broken).

He seemed to be especially happy that I took the seat
next to him rather than sitting in the back of the car. This way
it was easier for him to talk. And did he talk!

He was a friendly man, beaming a broad smile, which
made his ears shake when he laughed. His features carried the
unmistakable characteristics of Arabic and Cushite influence.
His nose had a distinct kink, almost like the hunch of a miniature camel. From the original 32 teeth with which a person is
endued, about 6 or 7, at the most 8 were left. That added a
somewhat mummified, certainly picturesque touch to him.

His accounts of what happened "at this street corner" or
"in that building across the marketplace" were fascinating. I
felt as if I were receiving an instant, quick-fix type of history
lesson on the way to the hotel.

This 20-minute journey would have been a remarkably
enjoyable ride for me had it not been for that incident that
shocked me back into the reality of Africa and to my assignment on this continent.

Until now I had observed everything as if watching a
movie or reading a book: with interest but with remoteness,
gripped by the strange fascination of beholding a new country,
enjoying a taste of another culture while personally being re-
moved from its reality.

As I pondered and weighed all these impressions, we
stopped at a traffic light. My driver companion proceeded to
tell me that this was one of the only two functioning traffic
lights in the whole city.

As he continued to talk, the rain hammering, staccato-
fashion, on the roof of our car, a small face appeared next to
me at the window. The big brown eyes of an approximately
10-year-old boy were accentuated by his runny nose and the
rain running down his forehead. As he pressed his nose
against the glass, he lifted two arms in a begging motion.
Nothing unusual about that, except that where hands and fin-

gers belonged, I could see only two stumps, smoother than a clenched fist.

A dirty, torn T-shirt covered his thin body. The sad, anguished look on his face reminded me of a hunted animal backed up against a wall, unable to run free. These horribly disfigured stumps, where his hands should have been, waved at me in a grotesque manner. I rolled the window down, looking frantically for some money, but, not having changed any money at the airport, I found nothing in my pocket. Then my eyes fell on two coins in the open ashtray next to the gearshift. I took these two coins and carefully tried to insert them between the two stumps. At that moment the traffic light turned green, the driver jerked the car as he moved on, and the coins dropped to the street. As the car began to move away, I looked back and saw this poor creature on his knees trying to collect the lost coins with those leprosy-eaten limbs in the muddy surface of the road.

This picture stayed with me until we arrived at the hotel. No longer did I hear what the driver had to say as he continued to give me a rundown on the city. No longer did I have any interest in what my eyes beheld. I fell into a thoughtful, almost depressed mood.

How on earth could we bring relief? How could we turn this page in the history of Africa and start with a new one, a blank one, inscribing beautiful letters? How could we leave the ugliness of the present reality and exchange it for the glorious, God-willed beauty of a life that will hold a future for Africa's young generation?

Fifty-one percent of Africa's population is 15 years or younger. What shocked me that morning was the fact that this one, singled-out illustration represented untold millions of an almost-lost generation. War, land mines, disease, and other scourges have taken their toll and hang like a heavy mortgage—hardly serviceable—over the population.

I was quiet, as if in a trance, when I approached the reception desk to check in to my room. Having paid my driver, who thanked me profusely, I was now on my own again. I made my way to the coffee place, a very special venue in Ethiopia.

There in the lobby of the hotel sat those to whom I referred earlier. Unlike in a similar Western world hotel foyer, where businessmen or tourists would mingle, the representatives of different nongovernmental organizations congregate Buddha-fashion, sitting with crossed legs around a coffeepot. I wondered how long their talks would continue—for the next few months, for years, or possibly for decades? I knew they, too, wanted to be of help—everybody scrambles to assist. But the question is "How?"

Back in my room, I took my Bible before hanging up my clothes. I wanted to reaffirm my assignment. I wanted God to give me a fresh reminder of my mission, calling me back to the task. So I searched for a way to receive heavenly reassurance. I wanted to be sure that my feeble attempts to help, my pangs of conscience over having it so much better, these nagging, intruding doubts about a hopeless situation, would be no more than fleeting temptations to do something that was so obviously small in the midst of formidable odds.

I needed to hear from God. I did not want to be reduced to become one of these people in the lobby who sincerely meant to do good but whose only equipment consisted of good intentions. I needed to hear from the Lord that indeed there was a remedy, a solution.

And so with the picture of that little boy at the traffic light before me, I waited before the Lord. All of a sudden, He seemed to say, "'Not by might nor by power, but by my Spirit,' says the Lord Almighty" (Zech. 4:6).

It sounded so clear, almost audible to me. Not by any other means, but certainly—definitely—by His Spirit. *Thank You, Lord!*

I read on about the mighty mountain of which God comments: "What are you, O mighty mountain? . . . You will become level ground. . . . [And there will be] shouts of 'God bless it! God bless it!'" (v. 7).

As I continued, I found confirmation: What Africa needed first and foremost was the hand and the Spirit of the Lord.

We have seen the might of great armies; we have experienced the power of the human mind—both of which ultimately brought little more than exploitation of this continent's great resources: man and material. We need the Spirit of the Lord.

The only thing missing in this equation seems to be the "Zerubbabels" of our time. God works through people. He seeks ministers and servants whom He wants to shape into leaders of His army. "The hands of Zerubbabel have laid the foundation of this temple; his hands will also complete it. Then you will know that the LORD Almighty has sent me to you" (v. 9).

God was talking to me in a very personal way: *I have laid My hand on you as I have laid My hand on many others . . . Therefore, go and teach . . . and make disciples . . . and remember: I will always be with you, until the very end of the age.*

My resolve was strengthened. I want to be found obedient, willing, joyfully trusting God for the really big things He wants to raise. He wants to build His temple, and He wants to build it through me.

Lord, help me to be equipped with Your Holy Spirit. Don't let me be so foolish as to try to trap Satan with what is of no avail. Help me not to attempt to catch a buffalo with a mosquito net, but to move in the power of Your Spirit. In Jesus' name I pray. Amen.

9
A Christmas Message in August

*It is when you are prepared to share
that you discover it is you who receives.*

$\mathcal{O}$ur destination was Quelimane, the old Portuguese trading port on the shores of the Indian Ocean in Mozambique. However, we could not bypass and overfly Mocuba without at least making short contact with our people there.

We were late flying in that day. Our visit in Mocuba, out in the wilds of Mozambique, had taken longer than anticipated. We had intended to only pop in for a short visit to get an idea of how the church in these areas, land mines abounding, refugee saturated, was doing. I was accompanied by missionary Ken Walker, Rev. Jonas Mulate, and our pilot.

The reception in Mocuba Village, approximately five miles out of the little war-ravaged town, was tremendous. The village headman and the pastor headed up the reception committee. The rest of the village population followed as we were led to the community guesthouse, a hut approximately 40 feet long and 20 feet wide. It served as the gathering place for important events.

I was offered a seat in the chief chair, a piece of furniture very cleverly built in two interlocking panels, the bottom about nine inches above the ground. I marveled at the architecture of the building. It was built with wooden poles, elephant grass, and reed stalks, all held together by homemade sisal ropes. The palisade was only about three feet high, the poles extending for another six feet and holding the grass roof. Only the two short sides had reed walls joining up with the roof. This way there was shelter from too much wind, while a welcome breeze on warm days would gently drift through the hall. Warm days and hot days were the norm.

A young lady with a towel across her forearm brought us a dish of water so we could wash our hands in true African style. Then we were served cornmeal porridge, bananas, and fried chicken. The generosity of the people was overwhelming. They had so little, and yet they shared what they had. As we chewed on the chicken pieces, I thought about the poor creatures, who probably had served as egg producers and breeding hens for many years before their final destination on our dinner table. I could not help but smile at the thought that they must have been ancient by the time they found their way into the cooking pots.

After the meal we heard a number of speeches. Then I was requested to hold a service in the village church. You had better be prepared to preach at any time in Africa! The time of day doesn't matter—early in the morning, noontime, or late at night.

We went down a little ravine, and there at the edge of the village was the mud-brick church building, which held approximately 200 people if properly "packed." Approximately 500 followed us. That, however, was no problem to the pastor. He organized everybody outside, let the important people enter the building, and started a song service. This went on for about one hour before we were given a 20-minute introduction, after which I was invited to share the Word.

The visit in Mocuba was as sweet as it was important. But it really sabotaged our plans to get to Quelimane on time. We weren't sure if word of our plans to come to Quelimane had reached there—no telephones, no faxes, no cars. You rely on the faithfulness of messengers, giving them plenty of time to help plan anything.

When we touched down very late that afternoon, we found no one at the airfield. Our people must either have been there and left after waiting for hours, thinking we would not come, or they had never received word of our plans.

What now? We began walking toward town, and eventually the driver of an old, beat-up truck mercifully let us climb into the back and took us on in. We found a small hotel and checked in for the night. After a refreshing glass of water, we held counsel among ourselves. Should we try to locate the church? It was getting dark already. Only Jonas knew approximately where to find the church. He told us, however, that he was not sure if he could find it in the dark. Furthermore, it would also mean about an hour's walk from where we were. After some discussion, we decided to try.

Again, not knowing what would await us, we took a camera, our Bibles, a bottle of water, our passports and wallets, some mosquito spray, and trudged out into the bush.

Quelimane—my thoughts raced back in history. Even now, as the sun was about to set, we could look across the exotic little bay that opened up toward the Indian Ocean. Some of the shoreline buildings were pretty old, probably reaching back 100 years or more.

This was the place where David Livingstone arrived in 1855, having crossed the African continent from the Atlantic to the Indian Ocean. It took him one year, eventually coming up the river by canoe, to reach Quelimane. How must he have felt to behold the gentle waves slapping the beautiful white beach, the ocean losing itself in the sparkling distance?

How many times had I crossed and recrossed some of the stops, routes, and camping places of the great explorer and those of others like him? It had taken Livingstone four years from the time he left Cape Town, making his way to Luanda, Angola, in the west and then crossing the continent, battling against many odds, eventually arriving in Quelimane.

On that trip he became the first white person to behold the famous, magnificent Victoria Falls. The existence of the falls had been known for some time from references of local tribes who spoke about "Mosi oa Tunya," meaning "The

Smoke That Thunders." These rumors had inspired great interest, and Livingstone decided to continue from Kalai by boat
in order to investigate it. He traveled down the great Zambezi
Valley, saturated with game—and malaria. He would sometimes move on foot, sometimes being carried by his faithful
Makololos and sometimes riding on a rather unpleasant ox,
"an animal of vicious manners named Sinbad." The Makololos
following behind him with their loads, as Ransford describes it
in his book *Livingstone's Lake,* "vastly intrigued by this white
magician whose legs were wrapped in bags, and in doing so
giving a new word for trousers to the English language."

It had been my privilege to be in Tete, Mozambique,
where he stopped, this being the last outpost of the white man
in East Africa. I had experienced the thrill of visiting Blantyre
in Malawi, Lake Malombe, and Lake Nyassa, today called
Lake Malawi. This great freshwater lake, 50 miles across and
300 miles long, also discovered by Livingstone, marks the
great divide of the continental shelf, later becoming the famous Rift Valley, stretching from the Red Sea in the Northeast
to Mozambique in the Southeast, on the way creating the
Great Lake region.

I had followed and tracked the mighty Zambezi River and
the Shire River by plane, was fascinated by the multitude of
hippo populations and the sheer size of crocodiles in these
waters. And now I was here in Quelimane, the end of Livingstone's journey across Africa where the queen of England had
sent one of her cruisers to bring him home and to make him
the celebrity he became.

What a privilege to walk in the footsteps of such great
history-makers! I reminded myself that three years later the
British Foreign Office appointed Livingstone to the official post
of "Her Majesty's Consul at Quelimane, for the Eastern Coast
and the Independent Districts of the Interior." And now we
were here. Once again, it almost felt that we were treading on
holy ground . . .

By now the African night had dropped like a big black
curtain onto the stage of life. When it gets dark in Africa,
everything becomes black, and it happens so quickly. No
streetlights, no electricity—only an open fireplace here or

there, flickering flames lighting up dark faces. There's something beautiful about the silence and the solitude of Africa's night. Typical bush sounds abound. Birds find their nesting places and calm down. Crickets, on the contrary, wake up and pierce the night with their sharp, pointed, never-ending chirping. A bullfrog here and there croaks in deep bass that almost sounds like a distant roar. The stars shine brightly and vividly, providing a faraway but very real backdrop of splendor over the vastness of the land.

The Southern Cross, a fascinating constellation of stars in the form of a cross, points lost travelers to the true south on the horizon. It is a solid and dependable sentinel and a stark reminder of another cross, which also looks down upon earth, desiring to cover a troubled world—the cross of Jesus Christ.

We're now walking single file on a much-used path. Land mines are still around, remnants of a cruel war, planted without pattern, intended to instill fear and to destroy life. We're making our way toward the center of the village, having found a guard at the edge of the forest who said he knew where the Nazarene church was located. At last we began leaving the lonely bush path behind us, and it was there where Africa confronted us again in explosive expression of naked and undisguised truth. Two startling incidents set the mood for the evening.

Jonas had just asked one of the villagers if our direction was right when I saw a strange movement out of the corner of my eye. Half-human, half animal-like, it seemed to hop in unusual fashion, wanting to go, yet half constrained. Startled, I shone my flashlight in the direction and recognized a boy between 10 and 12 years of age, legs blown away by a land mine, supported only by his arms and hands, lifting his body a few centimeters off the ground and throwing it forward again and again.

The boy looked up, his big eyes squinting as the beam of my flashlight fell upon his face. What do you say, how do you react, what do you do in a moment like this? A torrent of emotions flood your soul. You want to help. You want to do something! But what? How?

I, too, am a father. I, too, have children. We stood in silence for a few minutes, watching the boy hopping away over the crusty surface, disappearing in the shadows of the night. Stunned for the moment, each one busy with his own thoughts, we continued our walk.

We had not gone but five minutes when a girl, approximately 14 years of age, stepped out of the bush ahead of us, making her way also toward the huts and houses. While I would have been too embarrassed and too ashamed to take a photograph of the boy without legs, this time I did.

The girl carried a rusty bucket full of water on her head through the night. Of course, this was nothing unusual in itself. Girls have to carry water sometimes for up to six and seven miles. What was different about the water supply was the fact that this bucket had a hole near the bottom, and water squirting out at an angle like from a fountain. The girl held an old paper cup in her hand, catching the stream of water pouring from the bucket and emptying it back into the bucket each time it was full. This picture has found a place in my Bible as a steady reminder how good I have it. It reminds me also that I am obligated, mandated, and compelled to share my abundance.

"I tell you the truth, whatever you did for one of the least of these brothers of mine, you did for me" (Matt. 25:40).

The scene changed very suddenly. We made out a group of people about 50 yards ahead, standing in front of a small mud-brick building and singing the song that Christians in Mozambique love to sing. Although this was not their language, they sang in Shangaan: "Yi Fikele Evangeli"—"The Gospel Has Arrived." Beautiful, almost angelic, complete harmony! What a soul-satisfying sound in the night of an African bush village.

We had found our church and learned that these good people had been waiting for us since noon. They had found no practical way to get to the airfield, so they had sat and sung and prayed and believed that somehow we would make our way and find the village, find the church—and there we were, and there they were.

At times like these you walk as in a trance. Am I dreaming? Is it all real? Can this be? Coming from a world of computers, traveling in jet aircraft at almost the speed of sound from country to country, driving a big automobile, having two television sets, sitting down in a beautiful restaurant being served T-bone steaks grilled to perfection, moving in and out of high-rise buildings beautifully designed and constructed of steel and stained glass, sharing air-conditioned offices—and then this! Another world, and yet this had become my world too.

We were led into the darkness of the sanctuary, under the banana leaf roof without windows. The pastor, a man who reached only up to my shoulders, led me by the hand through the darkness. Jonas, Ken, and the pilot followed me as I stumbled to the front.

We found our place on a crudely carved bench just behind what was to be the pulpit. We still could not see anything, but we were very much aware that the little church building was at capacity with people who had streamed in after us, still chanting and singing.

When everybody had more or less settled down, somebody struck a match, and three candles were lit: one in front of the pulpit, one to the right, and one to the left. There were about 140 people inside the room, with many more standing outside, trying to listen to what was going on.

As the pastor began the service, I realized that I would be unable to either read a scripture or see a sermon note. The three candles would only faintly light my face, and I would speak into stark darkness, not knowing who was sitting in front of me.

My thoughts raced—what could I tell them? What could I bring, preach, and share that would be meaningful and encouraging to these good people? I wondered how many of them were men and how many were ladies. How many young people were there, and how many children? What did they or did they not know of Jesus?

While I was thinking and quietly praying to the Lord to give me the right words, in the darkness I felt the pilot spraying my ankles with mosquito repellant. Only then did I become aware of the countless mosquitoes that seemingly had become alive, attracted by the three candles around the pulpit.

At last it was my turn. I then felt that I had a word for the congregation. The candles had inspired me, and I took a Christmas text, Isa. 9. Preaching in Africa at the most unusual times, often totally unexpected and frequently in the dark, one must be prepared, and it helps also to know scripture by heart.

I began, "The people walking in darkness have seen a great light; on those living in the land of the shadow of death a light has dawned. You have enlarged the nation and increased their joy; they rejoice before you. . . . For to us a child is born, to us a son is given" (vv. 2-3, 6).

I felt inspired with the reassurance that God had relied on me. I shared about the light that Jesus had brought. I shared about His love and the fact that the person who receives Him will no longer walk in the darkness of sin nor in the shadow of death.

I then illustrated by telling them about Christmas Eve services in my church when I was pastor in Frankfurt. I recounted how our young people would always specially prepare for that great evening, December 24. On that day every church in my country is filled with people. Christian and non-Christian—they would all come to the church service. This is true for all of Germany in every denomination.

Our young people would prepare red Christmas candles with white plaster of paris and a little pine twig sprinkled with silver gloss so as to indicate snow. Each person would receive a candle upon entering the sanctuary. Then at a certain moment during the service, we would turn the big lights down—I explained electricity and the lights in the church. The pastor would then light his candle and pass the light on to the first person in the choir, demonstrating how the light of Jesus should be shared. That person would pass it on to the next, and so on. From the choir the light would spread to the first pew and there again from one to the other. As the people one after another would have their candles lit, singing "Silent Night! Holy Night!" the darkness of the church would be dispelled as light would spread throughout and fill the sanctuary.

heard a lot of "oos" and "ahs," typical
and sounds of surprise and awe. I felt that
erstood the message.

beautiful service. The three candles in
wly burned down, by now much shorter
arted. We made our way back again into
frican night as we left the little church
the pastor stood, smiling broadly from
appy man.

ed to different people and as Brother
back and forth, I made a rather star-
d that the ecstatic sounds of surprise in
so much the result of the content of
ore expressions of unbelief and in-
at there could be a church so wealthy
could each have a candle and be able

As we left among heartfelt good-byes and even tears that
night, I felt that I had not been the one who brought the message, but rather that I had been the one who had received it.
Certainly my resolve to preach and share, to live for Christ
and tell His story, to thank God for what He had given me, became strongly reinforced. This, too, was my world, and I was
there in Christ's stead.

Back in Quelimane late that night, as we sat and shared a
bottle of mineral water with each other, we talked about that
day. Once more we recalled David Livingstone and his first
visit there in 1855. The words from his journal (October 30,
1843) came to mind. I quoted them as we prayed before we
went to sleep: "I shall try to hold myself in readiness to go
anywhere, provided it be forward."

10
A Brush with Death

As sure as the LORD lives and as you live,
there is only a step between me and death.
—1 Sam. 20:3

*S*outh Africa had become a rather unsafe place during the late 1980s. World pressure against the apartheid regime of the country made itself felt on just about every level. The cry to release Nelson Mandela from prison and the plea to recognize him as the leader of the liberation movement headed by the Africa National Congress became increasingly louder. Insurgents from abroad, or freedom fighters, so called on the other side, made continuous raids into the country, laying mines on farm roads, blowing up electricity pylons, and going after other strategic targets. The South African Defense Force, on the other hand, made commando raids into neighboring countries like Botswana, Zimbabwe, and Mozambique.

Life within South Africa was changing rapidly. People were arming themselves. Politicians slugged it out with big speeches to parliament and in the streets of cities by walking with strikers. Labor unions became more aggressive as the Africa National Congress called for unrest and boycotts to make the land ungovernable. This was the time when *toy-toy*, a rhythmic dance on one leg changing from left to right, with the other leg angled up in the air, arms waving, became the African-style protest language of the people. It could daily be seen on television screens, in news reports, and in front-page newspaper photos. The nation held its breath. Sinister schemes were expected at every turn. Suspicion was ripe, and while everyone knew that something was in the air, nobody knew what that would be and where it would lead. It was not a pleasant time to live in the country.

The Africa Regional Office of the Church of the Nazarene in Johannesburg did everything to calm missionaries and to fend off any panic where it seemed to pop up. In spite of this, however, a number of our missionaries packed emergency rations, had extra fuel in the garage for their cars, and kept suitcases packed should a sudden and hasty retreat or escape become necessary.

I had a near brush with death at that time. To this day I ascribe my survival only to God's intervention.

I had flown north to Thohoyandou, which was then the capital city in the homeland of Venda. It bordered on the country of Zimbabwe, divided only by an electric fence, the mined 10-meter corridor, and the Limpopo River, all three of which formed the national border of South Africa.

Having met with the church people in Venda and completed my stay there, I still wanted to touch down on a small airfield to the north, where two of our churches were located. I landed there in the afternoon in my Cessna 206 and found a ride to the nearby town, the center of a farming area. Our people needed encouragement. They needed to know that the international church had not forgotten their plight and that the regional office was functional.

It was about a three-and-a-half-hour flight back from there to Johannesburg. I met with the pastor of one of the two churches, and he and a lay brother took me back to the airfield. However, as is not unusual in the summer months of Africa, the sky in the west became darker and darker. That was the direction of the airfield. One of the summer thunderstorms was building up, the rising cumulus clouds forming anvils. Such storms in this part of the world can be very severe, with hail as big as tennis balls. I was afraid for my airplane, and I wanted to make the landing strip before the thunderstorm struck so I could take off and get out of there. As we came closer, with lightning striking all around us, I saw that we were entirely too late. Once more we checked the ropes with which I had tied the aircraft down to make sure they were secure. Hoping for the best, that any hail would not damage the wings, I breathed a prayer and decided to ride back to town with our two brothers. It looked as though we would have to wait an hour or longer for the storm to pass, and that would make me late for my flight to Johannesburg. So I accepted the invitation to spend the night.

A frugal meal, warm fellowship, the sharing of experiences, and short evening devotions sweetened the day. I planned to leave at daybreak the next morning.

The night was filled with lightning. Thunder rolled and reverberated. The storm circled for hours before it left the area. Sleeping through such a storm in a grass-roofed hut can be scary. Many times, during the summer months, huts like these are struck by lightning, and South Africa's statistics of deaths by lightning strikes in villages around the country are frightening.

Just before daybreak, my host awakened me. I had a refreshing wash outside, and then a cup of coffee and a piece of bread with jam helped me look forward to the day.

We said good-bye and left for the airfield, approximately seven kilometers away. As we came closer, however, we saw a lot of people in the usually quiet, lonely farm fields, especially so early in the morning. We soon saw that they were soldiers with military vehicles. We stopped at the roadblock, and an officer came to the window.

"And where would you be going so early in the morning?" he asked.

"We want to reach the airfield over there. I landed my Cessna there yesterday, but I couldn't get out before the thunderstorm. So I decided to spend the night here. I'm on my way back to Johannesburg."

"Well, Sir, you won't be heading anywhere," the officer replied.

"How come—what's wrong? I see all of you here—are you in maneuver?" I asked. "I just want to take off, and you can carry on with what you're busy doing."

"You don't understand the gravity of the situation," he replied. "Leave your car here and come with me."

We parked the car and walked with him. There we learned a hair-raising story.

A giraffe had apparently strayed over the landing strip during the night and tripped a buried land mine there. The land mine had exploded and killed the giraffe. Nearby villagers had alerted the police, who in turn alerted the army. They had come out and found three more land mines on the strip. They were now busy cleaning it up, making sure that there were no more in the area. It would take several hours.

When we reached the airstrip and I saw the hole of the exploded land mine, I got goose pimples on my back. These explosives had been buried at the end of the runway from which I had made my approach. Fortunately I had landed deep and touched down approximately 40 meters behind it. I had brought my aircraft to a stop about halfway in the runway and then taxied to the side, where I tied up the plane. It was still there, neatly parked and unharmed.

The officer, now joined by two others who congratulated me on a miraculous escape, showed us where the other three mines were buried. With the prevailing winds that morning, I would have taken off in that direction. The detonating pins of these land mines had been wired so that instead of having just one point of ignition, the mine would explode if these wires would have been touched anywhere within a width of six to eight feet. It was clear to me that if the giraffe had not tripped that one mine, I almost certainly would have touched one of the other three on takeoff.

Yes, I was shaken, white as a sheet, but thankful to God for His incredible protection. The officer led me to a tent, where I had another cup of steaming coffee. We sat around for about two hours, just talking about the situation in the country, and it gave me good opportunity to share with these officers who I was and why I was there. They asked me to pray before I left.

As soon as I got the green light, I said good-bye, and off I went. Up in the air, I began to realize and fully comprehend how close I had come to saying good-bye to this earth.

I decided to keep the story to myself, except sharing it with my general superintendent, Charles Strickland. I did so at the time of his next visit to Africa, which was to be his last. I still hear his words, "Richard, promise me not to take any more chances. The church needs you to stay alive, and Valerie is not ready yet to be without a husband."

We had a little theological dialogue about the permissible will of God. I had responded to Dr. Strickland, with tongue in cheek, I confess, "If God still needs me here, He'll look after me." But then I also realized the wisdom of Dr. Strickland's remarks and accepted his guidance in taking even better precautions in the future.

God helped us to weather these precarious years in South Africa without casualties on one hand and without having any of our people, although scared at times, walking away from the responsibilities that God had entrusted to us through the church.

11
Scary Moments with a Blessed End

Yesterday's future is today's reality,
and the dreams of today are the hope for tomorrow.

In Mozambique after the mid-1980s the atrocities of a 15-year civil war had slowly begun to abate. Frelimo and Renamo, the parties at war with each other, had been responsible for over a million dead, thousands injured and mutilated, leaving a trail of people with limbs torn from their bodies by exploding land mines, noses and ears having been cut off in rage—humanity at its worst. News spread throughout the country that a truce had been struck. The nation was tired of war and bloodshed. People realized that ideologies could not feed hungry stomachs. Brutal force, enslavement, and horrific massacres brought neither joy nor enrichment to anyone. Tears, lament, emptiness, vacuum, nothingness—a broken nation bleeding from a million wounds.

While the images of open warfare slowly receded, there were still thousands of 10- to 15-year-old "child soldiers," wielding hand grenades, automatic rifles, and machetes, who had no home, no parents, no family ties. A lost generation born with no patterns or role models of peace, harmony, or the basics of normal life.

The people of Mozambique are by nature kind and warm-hearted, a welcoming people. I found them to be unusually diligent and industrious. Indeed, 15 years later, Mozambique is one of the success stories of Africa in terms of reconciliation, rebuilding, and the reshaping of a nation.

As the country opened its doors to non-Russians (Russian soldiers had been the normal picture in Mozambique during the civil war, since Russian military was very heavily involved in what was going on), the Church of the Nazarene began looking northward into this 2,000-kilometer-long country. Nazarenes in the capital city of Maputo, while decimated in numbers from the war, remarkably survived and were found to be strong in their faith. Committed church leaders had sacrificially continued to care for their flocks throughout the war years.

Although the Church of the Nazarene was strongest in areas tightly controlled by Communist rule, doctrine, and conduct, Nazarene families were known to be strong in faith, well-read in the Word, never giving up hope for a new tomorrow. They were a content and God-trusting people amid the chaos and carnage of what was left of the country.

But now we wanted to go north. Jonas Mulate, pastor of Citade Church in Maputo, and his family spearheaded the pioneering of these large areas, hitherto untouched by the church. The city of Nampula, 900 miles north of Maputo, was formerly a pleasant farm community with white, flat-roofed Portuguese villas. It served a fertile countryside with its ranches and farms during the colonial period. But now it was scarred by the war—sewerage systems dysfunctional, water reservoirs no longer in existence, streets torn up, houses with windows broken out, gardens bare of any fences, grass in the front yards overgrown to the point that snakes had the run of the terrain.

The first small Protestant congregation had been formed in Nampula. Young Nazarene converts were eager to be taught and trained; they hungered for the Word of God. The main cry of the people there was not for food, but for Bibles in their own languages. Since Nampula was still inaccessible by road from Maputo, I decided to fly a planeload of Bibles there and to meet with our people to encourage them to become part of a great evangelistic movement throughout northern Mozambique.

This was to be my first flight from Maputo to the north. I knew I was on my own in this area, where there was no navigational help, control towers, or weather reports—over 900 miles of hostile territory. My last refueling stop would be at Beira, the port city on the shores of the Indian Ocean, approximately 350 miles south of Nampula. It was a very long way for the Cessna 206 with its precious but heavy cargo of Bibles.

Winging my way over river basins and bushveld, I thought of Ken Walker, our committed field director for that area. Then I thought of the Mulate family, who had gone north without security, without salary, without budget—all they had asked for was the prayer and the blessings of the church as they went. What giants of faith on the frontline, virtually in the first trench of the battlefield! Truly, the Nazarene family is blessed to have such high-caliber leaders in her ranks.

I landed in Nampula on the small and rather short runway just outside the city limits. A lay brother from the church was there in a little truck that surely had seen better days. But being used to these kinds of vehicles in Africa—which never cease to amaze me with their seemingly unlimited power to still turn the wheels—we began loading the Bibles. All the while, Stephen, my companion, praised the Lord and repeatedly talked about receiving the Word of God.

Having tied up the plane, we now made our way toward town. We had hardly driven about 500 meters when we saw a boy standing in the middle of the road waving his arms. I noticed Stephen getting a little uneasy and wondered why. We slowed down, but Stephen was obviously looking for a way to drive around the boy. The road was not very wide and had steep banks on both sides, and it was obvious that the boy in the road was not about to move. We stopped, and he came up to my window. I turned it down and heard Stephen softly, almost under his breath, murmuring, "Be careful, Doctor—boy no good."

I looked into the face of about a 13-year-old, with a band around his forehead, a ragged brown shirt, shorts, and barefooted. He did not smile and showed none of the respect that a normal Mozambican boy would have displayed.

"Leave the car—come out," he said in Portuguese. It became clear to me then that something was not right. Suddenly, as I opened the door, I saw that he had a machete in his hand, having pulled it out from a sheath on his back behind his head.

I was now soundly alerted and, always traveling in Africa with a flick-knife in my pocket, I moved out of the car thinking that this kid, even with a machete in his hand, would not be a big problem for me. I heard Stephen mumble something on the other side but took no notice of him, keeping my gaze fixed on the kid while I slipped my right hand into my pocket.

Just as my feet hit the ground, however, a movement came from behind a 10-foot-high anthill about 5 meters from the road where two more kids emerged. One moved to the left and the other to the right, both pointing AK-47s at us. They did not look like jokers.

"Richard," I thought, "you really ran into this one without much thinking." I lifted my hands way above my head, as did Stephen. As they came closer, one of them, approximately 20 years old, started up a conversation with Stephen in Portuguese. Stephen translated that they wanted my watch and any money I was carrying with me. I asked Stephen if he thought we would get out of this situation if I gave them what they asked for, to which he answered that he was not sure but thought we might.

I now commenced to strike up a conversation through Stephen as an interpreter, explaining to them who I was and what we were doing, while pointing at the load of Bibles at the back. At first they appeared to be not very interested in or impressed by anything I had to say. But then the oldest walked around the vehicle. Stephen opened the back and took out one of the Bibles, which were written in Portuguese and two local languages. He took a few, put them into the big side pockets of his khaki pants, and came back.

By then, the boy with the machete had sheathed his weapon and commenced to take the watch off my arm and then searched my pockets for money while the third boy still covered us with his rifle. I had a few meticaix (Mozambique currency) in my shirt pocket to the value of about US $150. That quickly disappeared. He found the flick-knife in my trousers, tried it out, motioned to the other two as to what he had found, laughed about it, and put it in his belt. He relieved me further of a small handheld compass, my shoes, some mints, and a bottle of water. Then he stepped back. I wondered what would come next.

More conversation ensued between Stephen and the oldest, apparently the leader of three. I could make out enough to understand what Stephen was telling them—for instance, that I came from Germany, that I was a preacher of the Word, and that I was here to help people. Suddenly they motioned us to drive on. We got back in the car, and off we went. About 50 meters down the road I turned around—all three had disappeared.

How thankful we were to be alive! I was also grateful that I still had my briefcase with passport, documents, United States dollars, and a lot of other important items (I always said that I carry my life in my briefcase). It was still in the back of the car, covered by all these Bibles. Still shaken by this experience, we rejoiced over God's protection. After a while, when it struck us that we had looked into the barrel of an AK-47 and were now still sitting there, I without my watch or shoes and Stephen without a belt, the whole situation struck us as very funny, and both of us began to laugh. It was an expression of relief, no doubt. As Stephen continued to drive, I offered a brief but joyful prayer to the Lord and heard a repeated "Amen" from Stephen. Then we arrived in town.

There was great excitement among the people when they heard about our ordeal. However, I sensed that this was not a very unusual experience for them, so I tried to put it behind me. I still chuckle today when I think of how I preached to them that day standing behind that self-made pulpit with jacket and tie and only in socks—no shoes—and imagine that even the angels in heaven had a good laugh at this eager servant of the Lord. To this day I wonder why these bandits didn't take my jacket also. Nevertheless, I knew that God was still on the throne and in full control.

It was about two years later when we planned a return trip to Nampula. By then we had regional missionaries pastoring the church there—a fine young family, the Monteiros, from the Cape Verde Islands. The congregation had grown considerably, and the Monteiros were busy building a sanctuary. On that trip we had a pilot (our aviation program in Africa was now taking off, and the church owned two airplanes already, a Cessna 206 and a Cessna 210). Jonas Mulate and field director Ken Walker accompanied me. As we drove by the old anthill on the way to town, I recalled the previous experience. Things had changed considerably since then, and roads were much safer. Signs of the war had faded away.

What a beautiful reception we got from our people in Nampula! The Monteiros were happy to see us there. Pastor Daniel proudly showed us his church building, which was up to window height but still without roof, without doors, and without pews. A few corrugated iron sheets covered the platform very sparingly to provide shelter from the burning sun. These sheets were dangerously placed on very thin branches about five meters above our heads. *Lord, just don't let the wind blow!*

What a service we had! The church building was filled with people, sitting on the floor, standing through the entrance, even outside.

It became a most unusual gathering but full of joy and exuberance. Daniel is a very lively and enthusiastic pastor. He played the accordion, and he had people singing so loudly that the Catholic priest in his church about 300 meters down the road could not be easily heard reading his mass.

Daniel had a very unique way of involving everyone in his service. What we didn't know was that we were to become the "victims" of a very special scheme. It all centered on an offering for further work on his church.

Daniel led the singing with his accordion. Two men placed a basket the size of a small table in front of him. After a while, Daniel gave a speech asking all the "mamas" in the congregation to come and bring their offering. While the people chanted and Daniel played, the ladies in the church started a slow, rhythmic dance down the aisle to the front, where they placed their offerings in slow motion, almost staccato-style, into the basket. As we sat on the platform, we motioned to each other that we could not just let the ladies make a donation—although thinking that this was the custom here. So, we got up and put our share in the basket too. After all, it was for the Lord and for the completion of the building.

After the ladies had danced back to their seats, Daniel started up again. "We have so many children in the church," he said. "Let's give them a chance to bring their offerings."

Again, the congregation started chanting, and the children started their own little dance down the aisle to the basket. I leaned over to Brother Ken and said, "I think we need to encourage these kids and put another offering in." So we got up again and placed a second donation into the basket. Having completed their task, the children danced back to their seats. Daniel was up on his feet again and said, "This was beautiful. We had the mamas bring an offering, and we had the children bring offerings. Now let's give the papas in the congregation an opportunity." And yes, the whole ceremony started again, people chanting, Daniel playing his accordion, men dancing down the aisle to the basket.

Of course, all of us on the platform were papas also. So we had to make our contribution, thus making a third trip to the front. People applauded. The hall was filled with great happiness.

After the papas had danced back to their seats, I took my Bible. It was now my turn to bring the Word of God. How mistaken I was! Daniel got up again. Thanking the papas and thanking everyone else for their generosity, he prayed a special prayer to God to multiply what had been collected. But instead of now turning the service over to me, he addressed the congregation once more. It went something like this, with Jonas Mulate translating for Ken and me: "What a wonderful day God has given us! The sun is shining. Our families are being blessed. People in the community are waiting on what will happen with the future of our church. This day God has brought us these very special guests and visitors right out of the sky."

Everybody started applauding and shouting words of welcome in Portuguese and in the local languages. Daniel continued, "We have built our sanctuary up to window height, and all of this was done by Nazarenes of Nampula. Today you have given a special offering, our mamas and the children and our papas. I'm sure our guests would not like to be left out of the privilege of giving"—the rascal had seen very well that we had already given three offerings.

"Don't you think it would be unfair if we would not give that special privilege to our special guests. What do you say?"

He was interrupted by shouting such as "Praise the Lord!" "Welcome!" "Do it!" "Thank You, God!"—all in different languages. Daniel took his accordion, and once more the congregation started singing, chanting, and dancing while we on the platform made our fourth trip to the basket. It became a wonderful service, and God was very near.

The next morning was to be the first district assembly of the now 13 churches on the Nampula District. Because of the sun, we did not meet in the church hall, but behind it in an old building of clay bricks. The walls had cracks wide enough to reach through. Just as I did the day before in the church, I watched these walls very carefully and hoped for no wind. I also saw Ken observing with great suspicion the building with its crooked walls.

We started the assembly with devotions. As I was coming to the end of my morning sermon, reflecting on the service and the blessings of the previous day, challenging the congregation to trust God for great things, I suddenly saw a movement at the back of our little tabernacle. A man stood up. He had a long coat down to his feet, making his way forward to the pulpit. As he came closer—I was still preaching—I saw that he carried an AK-47 rifle in his hands. My heart started to race. The experience of my last visit arose before my mental eye, and I became silent.

By then the man had made his way right down to me. I almost did not trust my eyes. I recognized the oldest of the three bandits who had waylaid us on the road from the airport. I looked into his wet eyes. Slowly he stretched out his arms and placed the rifle on the little wooden bench that served as an altar. He reached in his pocket, pulled out my watch, handed it to me, and then knelt down to pray.

Can you imagine how God came upon our congregation? Others came forward, and I did not have to complete my invitation. People just came. They prayed. God blessed, and we concluded a wonderful first assembly of the Nampula District.

That experience is engraved in my memory. I understand that the young man not only found the Lord but, under the tuition of Daniel Monteiro, started out as a lay preacher and is today pastor of a small congregation in the port city of Ncala. God had again overruled. We planted a seed, and God grew a tree. We asked for a little, and God gave us plenty. We were happy to be alive, and God provided abundance.

We have a fine missionary in Nampula today, David Mosher. His initial years there in the area read like the Book of Acts. There have been times when he walked 10 kilometers or more through the sand to baptize as many as 400 new converts in the river. Revival fires have swept the area, and God continues to build His kingdom.

12
Slave Station—Outpost West

Where selfishness, greed, and nepotism reign,
the inevitable result will be losers with no joy,
cowards with no hearts, victims of lost causes.

*I*t was a hot and humid West African Saturday morning when I got up. Little did I know that it would heat up much more that weekend—and I'm not referring to the air temperature.

About two hours later, I found myself surrounded by perspiring bodies. The odor of man and beast in my nostrils, I tried to keep my feet firm on the deck planks of the ferryboat. Hopelessly overloaded, I mused, remembering the many ferryboat disasters in the Philippines and the Indian subcontinent the years before.

The engines began to whine, and a quiver ran through the rusty foredeck as the old ship struggled slowly away from the landing in Dakar, Senegal.

Our destination was the small island of Goree, a few miles out at sea and formerly the last station for slaves who were collected warehouse-style before their final gruesome journey to the New World into an uncertain future. Three hundred long years of trade in human merchandise was part of this island's legacy.

What an unforgettable picture presented itself to me that morning! It was the day before the great Moslem Reconciliation Celebration, which coincided in 1999 with the Christian Palm Sunday.

Early in the morning one could see and hear the collection of desert goats, males only, with ropes around their necks, as they were dragged through the dusty streets of Dakar, destined for ritual slaughter in front of every house the next day. The animal would hang from a tree or from a self-fabricated scaffolding, with the oldest boy in the family catching the blood from the goat after a quick stroke with a knife had slashed its throat. I witnessed these slaughters on the way to church the next morning. They were carried out in a macabre sort of dignity.

Goree Island was not to be excluded. It, too, would receive its quota for the day. And there they were, blaring anxiously, fear in their eyes, stiff-leggedly resisting the herdsmen who pulled and dragged them with ropes, others hitting the animals from behind in order to steer them over the small gangway onto the ferryboat.

In the midst of shouting and cursing, with the stench of urine, excrement, and dirty water filling the air, I once again asked myself, as I often do in similar situations, "Rich, what, for heaven's sake, are you doing here?" And I naturally answered myself, "I'm here 'for heaven's sake.'"

Senegal, West Africa, is "the nose of Africa," pushing itself out into the cold Atlantic—and then nothing but water for thousands of miles to the shores of North America.

We had no missionaries in Senegal at that time. I was by myself. But on that particular day, a Cape Verdean pastor and a young man from our embryo church in Dakar accompanied me. He became my interpreter, both for language and culture.

And then we stood in one of these despicable slave houses on Goree Island, preserved as a historic monument for future generations. Inside the cold limestone dungeon, rusted iron clamps still in the walls reminded me of the torture chambers in medieval European castles. One could almost inhale the stench of human depravity and decadence demonstrated here for centuries. Men, women, boys, and girls would be held there in squalid conditions, crammed together with not an inch of privacy or personal hygiene facilities. With little to eat and nothing to look forward to, they would be weighed, counted, and selected according to what was considered suitable merchandise—that is, those they considered able to withstand the arduous journey. They would board a schooner that had been stripped down to make room for this human cargo with a ruthless crew and would brave the storms of the North Atlantic on their way west. No regard for family ties or any other considerations—this was a freight of despair for the slave markets of the New World.

It's difficult to describe my emotions standing there where such suffering abounded—especially being the only white person surrounded by so many Black people. Yes, it indeed reminded me of the great halls of medieval castles: full of gloom, exuding hopelessness, instilling fear. There was only one stark difference: the small opening approximately three feet high and two feet wide, the Gate of No Return, as they labeled it. Through this gate, one by one, these innocent people were forced to make their way over a plank to the lingering ship anchored just beyond, awaiting its tragic cargo.

That brought me back to the present. It was just one day before Palm Sunday. I thought of Jesus preparing to enter Jerusalem, the place where His sufferings were to culminate. I thought of the goats that were dragged on board the old ferry, destined for slaughter, and then the millions of Africans who, over three centuries, were forced through the Gate of No Return. Jesus went through His own Gate of No Return—but He went voluntarily.

Now, once more, my mission stood clear and unmistakable before me. I vividly recalled the reason why I was here. Now my destiny in Africa emerged again through the fog of many questions:

> To be a messenger of hope,
> An apostle of the Good News,
> A minister of the gospel.

"'I tell you,'" [Jesus] replied, 'if they keep quiet, the stones will cry out'" (Luke 19:40).

Lord, help me never to be silent when I need to speak out, never to be afraid when courage is needed, never to retreat when the command is to go!

What joy the next morning, when I stood in the pulpit of the little Nazarene church of Dakar, this island of Christendom in the Islamic ocean. Palm Sunday. Oh, how God helped me to preach about the coming of the Messiah, the entry of Jesus into the New Jerusalem, and particularly the entry of Jesus into the human heart!

One year later, the church is growing. We now have a missionary family there supporting the ministry of our faithful Senegalese Nazarenes.

God the Liberator has come indeed!

13
A Camel to
Last a
Lifetime

Put your foot onto the water,
and let God take care of the risk.

*A*ugust 1998. This was to be my last exploratory trip as regional director for the Church of the Nazarene in Africa. I have undertaken such trips from time to time, the first one during 1983 in East Africa. The purpose of these ventures was to "spy out the land" for the church to begin new work. I called them "Joshua ventures" after the exploration of Canaan, the Promised Land, according to Josh. 13:1—14:8.

These trips became the basis for opening the door in the different countries to allow the church to work and evangelize. As a result, we were able to pioneer the church in one country after another, growing from 8 countries in 1980 to 32 countries by 2000.

This trip was to a very special part of the African continent, the Horn of Africa. The countries around the horn are rich in history but abound with struggle as they attempt to incorporate into their fabric the manifold cultures whose exotic flavor causes them to compete with each other.

Djibouti, the center of it all, lies directly at Bab el Mandeb, Arabic for "Gate of Tears," named so because of the many shipwrecks in the narrow and shallow straits where the Red Sea squeezes in between two continents to be swallowed up by the great Indian Ocean.

Djibouti is a land of extremes. Like the Rock of Gibraltar, the most southern point of Europe, from which you can see Africa across the straits, so is Djibouti on African soil the rock from which you can almost see Asia across the narrowing Red Sea.

Djibouti is a very busy place, a blend of many cultures and a pivot of commercial enterprise and exchanges. Arab meets African. Muslim meets Christian. Asia meets Africa. Caravan routes from the north and the west make their way to the port of Djibouti. Greek and Chinese merchants engage in trade with Indian merchants, who in turn trade with Africans, exchanging incense, myrrh, kohl, ostrich feathers, and ivory carvings. This has gone on for many centuries.

The hustle and bustle of this port city intrigued and fascinated me. I wanted to get involved in it. Valerie, my wife, would have said, "Richard, you're sticking your neck out again—one day you'll get it chopped off." Indeed, I was about to stick my neck out again.

The second morning in Djibouti, I was about to signal for a taxi in front of my hotel. Strangely enough, there was no car, no taxi in sight—only drivers. They surrounded me, gesticulating and shouting in broken English, broken French, but mostly Arabic, trying to get my attention. The message was clear. Each was clamoring for my business. What do you do in a situation like this? I grabbed the hand of the one nearest to me and asked if he had a car. "One moment," he responded quickly in about three or four languages and then went off while the others continued pleading with me, a dozen hands so close to my face that I feared for my glasses and began a slow retreat. The driver who went for his car had a companion who now moved in, pushing back the competition, shouting in a language I did not understand. Then came the "taxi," a dented, beaten, scratched, hand-painted car with no lights, no bumpers, and, as I learned on closer inspection, only two front seats—yawning emptiness where the backseats were supposed to be. But that was not the worst. The car was being pushed by half-a-dozen barefooted lads with no shirts and only a pair of well-worn trunks on their skinny bodies.

Well, I thought, Africa being Africa, let's get down to business. I proceeded to negotiate the price for a trip to the harbor. That almost started a war. It was not just he and I in dialogue. A number of those who had been fighting him to get the business for themselves now sided with him and gave support to his outrageous bidding.

To my surprise, however, a group behind me supported my arguments with choral affirmatives of "Yes, please" in a howl of "Don't do it." The opposition countered my offers, and I soon realized that we were not getting anywhere except that the demeanor on both sides became more aggressive and uglier all the time.

Just then a young man, 28 years of age, as I learned later on, rescued me. In nice English he explained that he was the manager of the hotel and asked what the commotion was all about. I related the story, and he offered to take me down to the harbor for nothing—he had to go there anyway.

He got his car, and I chuckled at the sight as we drove past this contentious place where the two groups were still engaged in shouting at each other.

Omar—that was the young man's name—was a Jemenite from across the Red Sea, a devoted Muslim whose father, a trader, owned a dhow, one of the handmade wooden "miracles of the sea" that look as if they could not cross the river yet have traversed the oceans between Africa and India for a thousand years already.

Strolling around the harbor and taking in the noisy but colorful "to and fro" that makes up the oriental cycle of life, I saw a group of desert people with camels in the background, mats on the dusty ground, trading with Chinese sailors. I was especially impressed by a young boy who seemed to be acting as the interpreter. He had a brown oval face, a very pleasant smile, and a prominently curved nose that revealed his Semitic ancestry. I noticed that he was treated with respect by the older men, and I decided that I would engage him in conversation.

After a prolonged back and forth, the traders reached agreement with the sailors, who packed their newly acquired possessions of skins, carvings, and weavings and happily made their way back to the ship.

I motioned the boy to me.

"Hello, my friend. Did you do well in your business?"

"Oh, yes, Sir. Today was better than yesterday."

"What's your name, and where do you come from?"

"They call me Achmed. We are Afar nomads from the South."

Just then two of the older men came over. Not being conversant in English, they apparently asked Achmed what this foreigner had in mind. An interesting conversation developed.

I learned that Achmed had picked up his English through dealing with sailors at the harbor, that they were traders from a nomad village in the desert. They made their living by caravanning back and forth to supply their clan with modern utensils like brushes, tools, shovels, knives, and so on, in exchange for paintings, carvings, and weavings. Their mode of transportation was camels, and tomorrow they would make their way back to the village.

Just then, my adventurous spirit got the better of me again, and I spontaneously asked, "Would you take me with you?" They looked at me with astonishment, almost in shock.

"We are leaving early in the morning—it is a long way, and we either walk or ride on camels."

"That's all right," I said with a twinkle in my eye, but trembling on the inside. "We have horses where I come from, but let me try a camel."

We arranged to meet early in the morning at the lighthouse just outside the port. I found my driver again and went back to the hotel. I packed my emergency kit, took a change of clothes, wrapped my toiletries, and packed the little Ethiopian brass crosses that I had purchased in Addis Ababa. I put some dollar notes as well as Ethiopian birr into a secret pocket of my jacket and a special reserve into the inner linings of my belt, handed the rest of my money, credit cards, and passport neatly wrapped in leather to the hotel manager for safekeeping, and felt good.

After I shared all of this with Omar, the hotel manager, he tried to talk me out of the enterprise and probably thought that this German had gone out of his mind.

I did not sleep much that night. I did not want to miss my adventure, which was to begin at the unearthly hour of 2:00 in the morning. Omar, being kind enough to take me again, knocked at my door to take me down to the harbor lighthouse.

The streets were empty and silent. Even the many stray dogs roaming in the dirt and in the litter heaps along the streets during daytime seemed to be comatose—none was in sight. The town lay still, sleeping like a giant who would soon jiggle and wake up for another busy day.

We arrived at the lighthouse, and there they were: six camels loaded with shovels, pots and pans, tools and ladders, wheels and jerry cans, ropes and planks, and lots of bales and pads—who knows what they all contained?

There were a number of riding camels, one of which was brought to me. Achmed was so excited. He took me by the hand and said, "Good morning, Mr. Dactaar." (He had gleaned the title from the business card I had given him and, preferring it to my name, using it in such mutilated fashion that it caused me to laugh every time he looked at me with his contagious smile. He would put the emphasis on the second and third *a*'s and drew them out as if there were five in a row.) "We were wondering if you would really come."

"So was I until I got up this morning," I responded. "I'll rely on you, Achmed, to guide and inform me about what goes on. Always let me know what's happening."

In the meantime, I saw how the hotel manager talked to the other men, seemingly threatening them not to let any harm come my way. He was genuinely concerned. And then we were on our way.

I found myself seated on furs and skins strapped firmly to the smelly trunk of the animal. The up-and-down movements, first only a monotonous rocking but after a while an irritating shake-up of the body with abrasive friction in rather sensitive places of the anatomy, could be tolerated only by clenching my teeth. The distant but still audible morning prayer of the Muezzin reverberated from Djibouti's minarets, and our little caravan paused. My companions spread their colorful prayer mats on the ground and performed an indicated washing according to the dictates of the Koran by using the sand at their feet. Then they knelt down, forehead on the mat, reciting from memorized prayers. I had a chance to walk around, giving my limbs, stiff from the early-morning briskness, a little movement.

Needless to say, during the course of the day I repeatedly took advantage of any opportunity to get down off my camel for relief to my painful limbs. In the end I wasn't sure if I was seasick, if I had vertigo, or if I was close to a severe malaria attack.

By the time we reached our night camp 11 hours later, I was almost ready to walk back. If I had known the way (a map would not have helped, since there had been no landmarks and no roads), I would have done so. On the other hand, how could I give up?

That night, the furs and skins that had been my saddle were now my pillow. As I tried to fall asleep, I wondered, reflecting on the day, if that was indeed what God would expect of me in Africa. Was all of this part of preaching the gospel? Was this the price of my "Yes" to God's call? Oh, for an hour in the air-conditioned conference room of our World Mission office back in Kansas City, where ice-cooled soft drinks, celery sticks, carrot pieces, and grapes waited for consumption by conference attendees. Or for just one hour in my office in Johannesburg, leaning back in a comfortable recliner chair, feet on the desk, with a cup of coffee. But here I was, under Africa's skies, lying under a bush next to these men of the desert with whom I got acquainted only 24 hours ago.

It didn't help my sense of mission when I woke up the next morning and found a scorpion in my shoe. I gratefully thought about my friend, who taught me when I started my assignment in Africa always to check for these intruders before putting shoes on in the morning.

The next day was just as long and painful. Achmed tried to cheer me up and kept practicing his English on me. It end-ed at last when we saw the first people since our departure from Djibouti. We had reached our destination. We were in Somalia. No border post crossing, no customs officer, just sand and camels and my newfound friends.

But now a different picture presented itself: a number of black goatskin tents, each covering about 200 square feet with a low ceiling and one entrance. The population of the "village" consisted mainly of colorfully dressed women, completely covered except for their eyes. Children, suntanned and poorly clad, men, gray-haired with crooked noses and clothed in white caftans, made up the rest.

The whole village welcomed us with cheering, shouting, and laughter. I became the center of attraction and attention. Gazed at, touched by kids, surrounded by villagers, I felt like an artifact in a museum that had been taken out of the glass case.

The next few days passed like pages out of a storybook. They will remain engraved in my memory forever.

I lived with nine young men in one tent. Achmed never left my side. He became so attached that he was almost like my son. He explained, he translated, he looked after my well-being, he took time, he cared. His mother was a weaver. His father had hired on a ship from Djibouti and had not been home for over six months.

The food was simple, not created for Western tastes, but it was not unpleasant. We had two meals a day. I was taught the proper eating culture: sitting with crossed legs, weight on the left hip, using three fingers of the right hand. Couscous and rice fixed with tomatoes and green vegetables were the staple food. It was considered unmannered to just fill your mouth. One had to carefully work the food, kneading it into little round balls, dunking each in a sauce of goat fat with spicy meat and green leaves.

The means of hygiene were minimal. Water was scarce—it was not wasted on washing oneself but was needed for cooking. I walked with the young children, boys and girls, to the well. It was a kind of sand pool where the boys had dug a hole an arm's length deep. The girls scooped the water into plastic containers, careful not to let too much sand go with it. These were carried back to the tent village approximately half a mile from the water hole. The girls balanced the containers on their heads, one hand always trying to cover the face, lady fashion. When I offered my help to carry, the girls giggled, and the boys motioned "No" in disgust.

There were holes serving as toilets about 30 feet behind each tent and sheltered by a stick wall on three sides. The open side always pointed away from the tent. Depending on the wind, the smell could be intense and penetrating. I thought it fortunate that the camels were coupled close by— their aroma being more pleasant to my nostrils.

The most enchanting times were the evenings when the men sat around open fires, camel dung being the alternative to charcoal or wood. The latter, of course, was nonexistent, with almost no vegetation in the area. First were the evening prayers, and then dinner was served—about eight people around each pot, and then the happenings of the day were reviewed. I had a place of honor, always close to the sheikh, who, staff in hand, determined who would speak next. The women and children—perfectly quiet—remained in the background, listening to the jabber of the men.

The third evening, my last before heading back to Djibouti the next morning, offered me the opportunity I had been waiting for. By then I had gained the confidence of the people. I felt that they appreciated my being their guest—I certainly was privileged to break the monotony of their daily routine.

Each evening I had shared a little of my faith and of my work in assisting people in Africa and of how God guided and protected me. I had not told them that I was a preacher, only that I was a Christian.

That last night the old sheikh, Suleiman Habib, thanked me profusely for having "shared the tent" with his clan. I mastered all the courage I could find and told them if it was no offense I would like to leave a gift with each of them and proceeded to open the package with the little Ethiopian brass crosses and chains, of which I had bought about 150 on my way through Addis Abba. I knelt before my friend Suleiman

Habib and put one around his neck, then Achmed, and then the others as one by one they came to me. The whole clan received these crosses and proudly showed each other.

When I gave my little story about what it all meant, I had the full attention of all. Achmed was a star translator. It was then that old Habib said, "Thank you," with these words: "We wondered why you came through the desert to visit us. Your skin is white, but you have kind eyes and warm words. Allah is great, but the Allah you told us about is also giving. We must study the Koran to see if the Allah to whom we pray is also giving. The one we know so far only demands—thank you for your teaching."

I then had prayer for all of them (in German so that really only God would understand) and retired to my tent. Many sleepless hours followed. I twisted and turned as I reflected on my visit. Was I faithful to my calling? Did I say or do enough? Would God be pleased with my work?

We left early the next morning. It was, I admit, a tearful farewell. The whole clan was awake and waved good-bye. I knew I could not expect to see them again. They were nomads, moving every three to four months into new regions. No postal address. No certain way to contact them. Achmed clung to me until my camel started moving. He ran next to me for another half a mile or so. Then he just stood and wept and waved—and so did I—until I could not see him anymore.

My thoughts often go back to these people, and my prayers cover that young boy. God knows where he is—He always will.

Update: Missionary Howie Shute in Addis Abba, with whom I shared about my trip a week later, went to Djibouti and Somaliland for the first time three weeks thereafter. Today we have a group in Djibouti and a group in Somaliland meeting under the Nazarene banner, and many doors are opening in Muslim territory.

Yes, I know why I'm in Africa!

14
A Final Word

The African past lies in the belly of the termite, which has eaten all trace of past tropical civilizations. Let us beware that the African future does not lie in the bellies of self-appointed leaders whose interest is in no nobler cause but in that of their own bellies.

I owe much to Africa and still more to the people of Africa. Twenty years of helping to pioneer the church, to preach the good news of the life-changing power that comes from our Lord Jesus Christ, 20 years of helping to shape Africa in an impacting way can never be erased from what I am, how I think, and how I feel. God's overruling grace, anchored in His plan for humanity's salvation extended to the very least of us, has become an unfolding and ongoing discovery.

I find myself passionately in love with Africa. I do not only feel *for* the people—I feel *with* them. My heart throbs as I yearn for true liberation of soul and body, which, sadly, 40 years after the arrogance of colonialism was buried, has still to be achieved.

Africa pessimism is still very real in the West. It reminds me of Thomas Freedman's illustration about two Israelis discussing philosophy. One asked the other, "Are you an optimist or a pessimist?" The other answers, "I'm an optimist, of course. I'm certain that today will be better than tomorrow." This, generalized, is the perception of the world regarding Africa.

At the other end of the spectrum, however, the call for African renaissance that is being heard today, loudest in the

South but reverberated in the West, the North, and the East, has little or no foundation upon which a new future could be practically built. It's like a drowning man trying to pull himself out of the water by grabbing the neck of his shirt and saying to himself, "Let's go!" It will not work. The sad truth is that those in power of the nations of this continent, with very few exceptions, enjoy the plenty while Africa's population suffocates in the morass of greed and corruption radiating from the very same "high places."

Having traversed over 40 countries in these 20 years, with the church being established in 32, I testify to the scent of human poverty. As somebody has put it, "In temperate climates poverty smells sour, but in hot regions it is sickeningly sweet."

According to Paul Collier of the World Bank, only 15 percent of Africans today live in an environment considered minimally adequate for sustainable growth and development. At least 45 percent of Africans live in poverty, and African countries need growth rates of 7 percent or more to cut that figure in half within the next 15 years.

In the course of my work, I sat with monarchs, I dialogued with prime ministers, I dined with presidents, and I shook hands with dictators, suspiciously watched by gun-slinging bodyguards. I confess that I could detect little or no interest on their part in the destiny of their people.

I well remember that Saturday morning when the king of Swaziland was to attend the dedication of four new buildings at a theological college in Siteki. He had been announced. His office had made arrangements for the royal visit with the church's authorities. Brass plaques had been engraved with his name, the date, and the occasion, plaques solidly fastened to the walls that he was to unveil. Police cars with flashing lights were stationed along the route from Manzini to the east. Hundreds of boys and girls in their neat school uniforms with little Swazi flags in their hands had come early in the morning to stand along the sides of the roads during the last few miles up to Siteki, waiting for their king, prepared to welcome him.

Sadly, he never appeared. No word, no explanation, no apology. Two thousand people on the campus of the college postponed the beginning of the ceremonies for one hour, for two hours, for three hours—no monarch in sight.

I was there that morning. I could not help but wonder what impression this would leave in the minds of people, of the officials who had to dismantle the plaques from the walls again. What would these small children, who had so looked forward to this great day, take with them into the future of their lives?

A general superintendent of the Church of the Nazarene, Charles H. Strickland, was there. What did he think? What would he report overseas?

The Swazi church leaders who, according to tradition, had prepared that special breed of cattle, cleaned and adorned, that was to be presented as a gift in Swazi fashion to the king—did they have to take the cattle back to the corral?

If that had happened only once, one would probably have overlooked it and forgotten it. But sadly, such experiences became entry after entry in my diary.

Far be it from me to uplift the Western world as a role model for Africa. Corruption and greed are not confined to this continent alone. It's very basic to human nature everywhere. The difference? In the West, systems have evolved that provide checks and balances, in which people have a say and have a part in their destinies. I do not suggest that the Western world has the ideal solution—spiritual darkness prevails there as much as it does in Africa. The difference? Through almost 2,000 years of Christendom—with all the negatives, with even all the atrocities of the Inquisition, the debauchment of church leaders, the putrefaction of the Middle Ages, God triumphed, and a code of ethics emerged, a value system developed that, though admittedly late, allowed people to be people, creating systems of care and consideration and a nurture of communal interests.

That brings me to the core question: Is there hope for Africa? My unreserved and unqualified answer is a resounding "Yes!" If I had not been able to believe that there was, I would not have been able to endure and even enjoy the investment of 20 years in the wonderful people of this continent.

"The heart of the matter is a matter of the heart." Jesus Christ alone, the Word of God, the commitment and the dedication of sacrificial and selfless brothers and sisters, pastors and evangelists, church leaders and missionaries, will make the difference and help to steer the colossus of this continent into a new direction.

My heart is with the people. I consider them "my people." They are precious, eager, and willing. They do not need the patronizing and condescending demeanor of Western dignitaries. What they do need and what they deserve is our respect, our recognition, a place on the platform where they, with God in their hearts, abiding by the principles of His intentions for humanity, will become able to reestablish self-confidence, self-respect, and self-dignity in themselves. And not with cliché speeches and pompous state visits abroad, but with an attitude of "Let's do it!" they will roll up their sleeves and begin.

It is my conviction that our church, the Church of the Nazarene, has a very important role to play. The message of a pure heart and unselfish objectives, the message of our Lord's ongoing call for men and women, boys and girls, to submit to His reign is a mandate whose imperatives we cannot escape.

I also feel strongly that as we do our part and contribute to the shaping of this continent, expatriate Christians, hand-in-hand with indigenous leaders, brothers, and sisters, must jerk free from denominational littleness and narrow sectarian dictates so that people will be able to see the true Jesus, love sublime.

The next time people say to you, "We're stuck in an impossible situation. It's a dark tunnel, and when we look around, the only light we see is the train coming at us," your answer can be "Just step aside. Let the train pass so that you can see the bright light shining at the end of the tunnel, no longer hidden and obstructed by the train."

"A heart at peace gives life to the body, but envy rots the bones. He who oppresses the poor shows contempt for their Maker, but whoever is kind to the needy honors God" (Prov. 14:30-31).